G000022312

CONTENTS

FOREWORD

'Delightful', to be quite honest, is not a word I associate with books on personal evangelism. 'Earnest', 'serious', even 'instructive' come more readily to mind. But this one is different. Geoffrey Willis has written a truly delightful book. Indeed it is not only that, it is strategic too.

The delight comes from seeing an expert at work, and the real expert is a joy to watch – whether a fine athlete, artist, acrobat or author. Experts make things not only a joy to behold, but they often make them also look deceptively simple. Now some experts daunt us. It is a marvel to behold what they do, but it only underlines our conviction 'I could never do that'. Others are able to provoke in us the opposite response, namely 'I could do that!' Such is the effect of this book. It makes the work of sharing the faith both accessible and attractive. How does he achieve it?

It is the result of the author having a double expertise. He is not only good at sharing his faith with others, he is also an expert in helping others do the same. That is the sort of person it is good to have around, because he makes the subject accessible to all. He does so in several ways.

First, he removes unnecessary barriers. Somehow most of us have an idea that the only authentic way to do evangelism is either by going door-to-door to complete strangers, or by stealth with those you know all too well. Our picture of the latter is of steering the conversation round onto 'holy ground', by fair means or foul. Geoffrey Willis removes such false notions throughout the book. He also addresses all those artificial ways of steering conversations, button-holing people, and pushing our convictions on them. He is continually breaking out of stereotypes and the notion that evangelism is something stuck on to 'normal' conversation. One by one fears of unnatural or forced conversations are removed.

Second, he then makes all the right connections, showing how our own growth in faith and awareness of God can shape our sharing the faith in a natural way as the knowledge of God touches the whole of life: 'what you need to be effective in evangelism is nothing more or less than this; to be you', and 'evangelism means sharing yourself'. He has many creative and relaxed things to say about the many points of contact that life presents. I like particularly what he has to say about prayer and sharing of the faith. Although fewer than ten per cent of the population go to church, over sixty per cent pray. That is something that many people would like to know more about from those who practise it.

Third, he faces the cost. Delightful though this book is, it does not end up saying 'personal evangelism is the easiest and most natural thing in the world'. The author is too honest and experienced to make life that easy. What the book does manage to do, however, is to locate the real problems where they actually come from. Two he highlights are our reluctance to share ourselves – that is what hinders the sharing of our faith – and the loss of 'community' or connectedness with one another which is a sickness of epidemic proportions in our culture.

About the former (resistance to 'self-disclosure') he says: 'Being real is painful and costly.' Perhaps this is why so little real evangelism takes place. For here lies the real cost of evangelism. 'To be prepared to share yourself is to take a risk.' He then goes on to explore the reasons for that, and why and how we can break out of such imprisonment within ourselves in every area of life.

Related to this is the breakdown of community out of which natural opportunities emerge – 'our culture militates against our getting to know other people.' Again he has some wise things to say about the role of the Christian in such a culture, a role wider than, but including, the sharing of our faith.

However, I mentioned two words about this book in my opening comment. It is not only delightful, it is strategic, for one overriding reason. It is this: it comes, in the middle of the Decade of Evangelism, when a sea change has taken place in the Church's understanding and practice of evangelism. In a sentence, that sea change is the move from a 'crisis' understanding of evangelism to a 'process' model. The 'crisis' approach is concerned about 'making decisions', the 'process' approach focuses on 'making disciples'.

The evidence for this change is all around.

The development of such material as Good News Down The Street, Saints Alive!, Christian Basics (CPAS), and – more recently – the Alpha course, all are built around a series of sessions in which dialogue takes place as the natural location for evangelism. This change is much wider than the evangelical world and is evidenced by the renewal of the catechumenate (as for example in the Catholic Rite of Christian Initiation of Adults), and Cursillo weekends. It is an important and positive change. It is vital in our day simply because people need more information about the faith than previously when the background knowledge was greater. We are losing our Christian heritage. It is healthy because it enables people to learn at their own pace, rather than all in one go. The process approach is much more in tune also with the modern understanding of how real learning takes place – within a circle of 'experience – reflection – action'. It is also to be welcomed because it puts the work of evangelism back into the hands of the laity, rather than in the mouths of a few expert clergy/preachers.

Which is why *Won by One* is strategic.

As the number of churches moving into a process approach to evangelism increases, and various groups are set up as stepping stones for those making the journey into faith, so the number of church members involved in this process will increase. This book will be of particular help, for instance, to church members involved in establishing Christian Basics courses or Alpha courses.

Won by One is also strategic because in all this welcome change from crisis to process there is a hidden danger. It is that, as so often happens when a pendulum swing takes place in any area of life, we will end up with a 'process as *opposed to* crisis model'. That would be tragic. If coming to faith is a journey, it is obvious that there will be a number of 'crises', or turning, points on the way. Those making the journey will need people alongside them who can assist them in seeing the signs and making the right decisions. So this book comes at just the right time to help the Church develop a healthy and human way of assisting others at the 'crisis points' along the Way.

I commend it warmly. I am sure you will find it drawing you into, or on into, the sharing of your faith. It does so by removing false pictures, helping us to be real, to be ourselves, and thereby share the faith we have received with those whose lives we touch.

Robert Warren

PREFACE

I remember a meeting of the Parochial Church Council of the first church to which I belonged. Item five on the agenda was 'Evangelism' and the discussion was brief and inconclusive. Item six was 'A new coffee pot to use after the morning service'. Eventually the vicar interrupted the discussion and said, 'Why is it that the Church of Jesus Christ can spend forty-five minutes discussing coffee pots and only ten minutes talking about evangelism?' I didn't know the answer then, but I do now. The reason is that coffee pots are not frightening and most people have some experience of using them.

The vast majority of Christians I meet are put off by the word evangelism. They are frightened by the idea of it, and consequently run at the idea of getting involved in anything remotely evangelistic. I consider this quite normal given some of the gruesome techniques and stunts that have been used in the name of evangelism. If we are to enable normal Christians to spread the faith we must first convince them that evangelism does not have to be like the ghastly images that immediately spring to mind at the very mention of the word. Nor need evangelism be difficult, requiring lots and lots of training courses. In essence it is very simple. My hope is that the shy, retiring, faithful attender of an early-morning communion might find in this book a way to share their faith. A way which maintains their integrity and which involves no clever techniques.

I have had the privilege of working with all sorts of churches and all sorts of people in running evangelistic projects for Lee Abbey. It is the ordinary members of these churches that have proved to me that evangelism is not a specialist gift, but something in which literally anybody can be involved. This was most forcibly pointed out to me one night in Kingstanding in Birmingham. I had talked for almost two hours and was aware that we needed to draw the evening to a close. It would be a long drive back home to my community in North Devon. I had come up for the evening to meet with church leaders who were considering asking for our help in running an evangelistic mission. I wondered how my talk would go down, had I been a bit too pushy? I'm always aware that my enthusiasm for evangelism can give me verbal diarrhoea and I wondered if I had gone on for too long, but the group had seemed enthusiastic and I felt it necessary to give them as much information as possible so that they could decide whether they wanted to work with us on this mission project. I paused to let the vicar round off the evening. But a woman concluded it for us. What she said in two short sentences made me feel that I really had waffled, but it proved that I had got my point across. She summed up in these two short sentences our approach to evangelism: 'What you have been saying all comes down to two questions, doesn't it, really? Do you have a faith worth sharing? And do you have a friend worth sharing it with?'

So why write a 45,000-word book when the point can be summed up in only seventeen words? My only justification for the 44,983 additional words is the hope that in reading this book you will realize you do have a faith; that it is worth sharing; and that you might discover that there are ways you can share it with your friends.

1

MISSION IMPOSSIBLE

When I was little there was one television programme which I found compulsive viewing. I was thrilled when a few years ago it was repeated, not because I wanted to watch it again, but because it made such a perfect sermon illustration. It was called 'Mission Impossible'. The basic plot of the programme was the same each episode. Each week the team led by Jim was set the most impossible task. They might be challenged for example to remove all the gold bullion from the Bank of England during opening hours without anyone noticing, except that they were goodies and therefore the tasks were always honourable. You would then sit enraptured throughout the programme while they achieved the impossible. Every episode began in the same way. The gang leader would receive the job description which was prerecorded onto a cassette tape. He would sit and listen in silence to the most impossibly far-fetched description of the job to be done. The taped message always ended the same way: 'That is your mission, Jim, should you choose to accept it' and then the bit that particularly appealed to my adolescent mind: 'This tape will self-destruct in five seconds'. After the requisite pause the tape machine spontaneously burst into flames and melted in front of Jim and the viewers' eyes.

Jesus left His followers a job to do. The job description He gave to His disciples has been recorded not on a tape that destructed after a few seconds, but in the Bible, and has been carefully preserved for nearly two thousand years. The job description was considered so important that it was included in every one of the four Gospels, and also in the Acts of the Apostles. To Jesus' followers it must have seemed more far-fetched than the most implausible scenario portrayed in the 'Mission Impossible' series. In an age with no form of mass communication – before television, radio, and the invention of printing, let alone newspapers; without the benefit of rail let alone plane travel; and with the powerful Roman Empire and their own people out to get them, Jesus asked His followers to pass a message around the world. According to the account that Luke wrote in Acts 1:8 Jesus said to them:

> You will receive power when the Holy Spirit comes on you; and you will be my witnesses in Jerusalem, and in all Judea and Samaria, and to the ends of the earth.

How were they supposed to succeed in Jerusalem and Judea with their own people against them and the Roman Empire breathing down their necks, let alone reach the ends of the earth? To be told to 'go and make disciples of all nations'[1] must have seemed an impossibly tall order. Yet they did it. Or I could not have written this book and you would not be reading it. Think about it. The only reason you and I have a local church to attend is because those eleven men (eleven not twelve following the death of Judas) and the unknown number of women who also accompanied Jesus as His followers, obeyed His last command.

All too often evangelists or ministers try to encourage us to evangelize by making us feel guilty. The exhortation to evangelize is based around a sense of duty, and sermons all too frequently revolve around reminding us of our failed attempts to share our faith and the inadequacy of our witness, without any great help being offered about how we might overcome the obstacle of fear that so hinders us. I prefer to try and get people to evangelize out of a sense of gratitude. Not only out of the sense of gratitude that we should feel to God once we realize just what He has done for us, but also out of a sense of gratitude to those who passed on the faith to us. On the opening evening of my teaching weekends here at Lee Abbey I usually ask guests to chat with the person they are sitting next to and explain how they come to be at Lee Abbey this evening. I ask them to do a journey backwards, asking themselves the question: 'Who is responsible for me being here this evening?' Then in turn going one step further back; 'Who is responsible for my knowing or meeting that person?' By this means we often find out about the key people in someone's journey of faith. Pause and reflect for a moment. Who was influential in helping you to find the Christian faith? For many it will be parents who took us faithfully to church when we were little and something sank in. For some it will be teachers, for others ministers who were there when we needed them. In my own case it was the girl I subsequently married who challenged me to think through whether Christianity might be true. I remember my ACCM selection conference when the Church of England decided whether I was suitable to become a clergyman. One of the interviewers, an elderly canon, asked me to describe my Christian pilgrimage. After telling him about meeting Lucy and the huge impact she'd had, he replied: 'Do you realize how much you owe that woman?' I went home with a renewed sense of gratitude for the girl who passed on the Good News to me, and who by doing so, totally changed my life and gave me a sense of purpose. We should all be grateful for each and every one of those people who has helped our faith to grow. And out of this sense of gratitude should be born a desire to play our part in helping others to grow too.

The people who helped faith to be born in us are in some sense our spiritual parents. They are the mothers and fathers of our belief, the people who planted the seed of faith and who nurtured it into life. I have recently been trying to research my family tree – I've succeeded in getting back to the first decade of the last century and now know my great-great-great-grand-father. While doing my family tree I have often thought about my 'spiritual' family tree. I know who passed the faith on to me but who was responsible for passing it on to them, and who to that person and so on back? Like my real family tree I cannot get very far back in my 'spiritual ancestry'. But I do know one thing. If I could trace the chain of faith backwards through the person who brought faith to me, I would eventually get back to eleven men and a handful of women who obeyed that command and passed the faith on.

The Christian faith has been whispered down the generations, passed from person to person, and it has arrived at you and me. We stand at the end of a very long chain of people beginning with those who actually saw and touched God while He walked on earth. And it must not stop at me! When Jesus gave that instruction recorded in Acts, I do not think He meant that His disciples alone would pass the Good News around the world. I do not think He ever imagined one person carrying the Good News on their own. Rather the method implied in that command is much more like a chain reaction or a line of dominoes. I pass it on to you, you to a third person and they pass it to a fourth. That way the Good News can ripple outwards in ever increasing circles.

Evangelism (apart from the fact that it is not a game) is quite like Chinese Whispers. For those who no longer play games at Christmas (yet another catastrophic result of the television and video culture) allow me to explain. Chinese Whispers has its origin in an amusing if apocryphal anecdote from the First World War. A signals sergeant enters the General's office and rather apologetically says he has a message. When the General says to get on with it the sergeant says it is rather embarrassing. The General orders him to relay the message, whereupon the sergeant reports that the message from the front line is 'Send three and fourpence, we're going to a dance.' The General is furious and orders the sergeant to double-check the message. The sergeant soon returns red-faced to report that the message should have read 'Send reinforcements, we're going to advance.' Chinese Whispers involves getting a whole lot of people to stand in line. A message is whispered to the first who has to whisper it to the second and so on. The test is whether the message is faithfully carried down the line. The Christian message has been faithfully carried down the generations to us. My job as an evangelist is to challenge people to stand in line and to be prepared to pass it on. Sometimes Christians have acted like the spoilsport elderly uncle who despite all the coaxing in the world refuses to take part, protesting 'You don't really need me, I'm sure you can manage perfectly well on your own.'

The methods used to convey the message over the generations are legion. But what we need to know is what is effective in communicating that message today. We cannot afford to carry out our evangelism without assessing what is productive. If we are to evangelize constructively we need to understand exactly what it is that helps people to discover faith. Most current evangelistic strategies have been passed down from one person to another without anyone stopping to ask whether this is a good way to do it. We are scared to face facts and own up to the possibility that the reason our churches are emptying or declining is because our evangelism is ineffectual. It is time to realize that 'evangelisation needs to be founded on fact rather than fantasy'.[2]

A major piece of research has been carried out by John Finney, entitled *Finding Faith Today*. The biggest shock comes on the back cover which announces 'This is the first published research which explores how adults come to faith'. We need to make up lost time now that we have hard facts about just what is, and what is not, influential in bringing people to faith. We must examine our evangelism strategies in the light of this brilliant piece of research, and we must be prepared to change our methods as a result. We will avoid the conclusions of this research at our peril.

John Finney's research team worked with churches across the denominations in England with the straightforward goal of finding evidence about how adults in the 1990s come to faith. Over five hundred participants were asked, either in face-to-face interviews or by completing a twenty-two page questionnaire, about their spiritual journey and how it came about. The primary conclusion of Finney's report is crystal clear:

> It is likely that there will be no progress in helping someone to faith unless a basic human relationship has been established. Friendship leads to trust, and trust leads to a readiness to accept what the other has to say.[3]

This is the key to all evangelism: friendship. Sadly evangelism is all too often ineffective because it ignores this fact. Frequently our evangelistic strategies are based on methods that avoid the intimacy of close friends in preference to large-scale impersonal events. When you mention the word evangelism virtually everybody thinks of Billy Graham; large-scale crusades in football stadiums or marquees; or alternatively cold knocking on the doors of strangers. As John Finney puts it:

> In the popular stereotype, evangelism is big events, and to evangelize is to organize big events. This research shows conclusively that this is certainly not the only or even the main way to evangelize.[4]

Billy Graham himself has often pointed out that if he were to preach and convert 10,000 people every night with the world population at 4.5 billion it would take 1,233 years to convert the world. Whereas if in the first year one Christian were to help convert one other, and in the second year both were to convert one, and in the third year all four were to convert one each it would take only 32 years to convert the whole world. Such statistics are of course ridiculous, nevertheless they neatly make the point that the only really effective way to fulfil Jesus' command is for each of us to stand in line and be counted. The method of evangelism that Jesus ordained was personal, one to one, and for all nations to be reached, for it to spread to all people everywhere, it requires that all of us be prepared to play our part. It is not the preaching of the professionals that brings people to faith, rather it is the people sitting in the pews who are effective in passing on the faith to their friends.

But we live in an age which increasingly undervalues friendship. The prevalent doctrine of our age is individualism – look after yourself Jack and don't mind about anybody else. It is little wonder that elderly people have sometimes lain dead in their flats for weeks before anybody notices their absence. It should not surprise us therefore that it is difficult to proclaim the Gospel, for friendship is at the very root of the Good News. The aim of our proclamation of the Good News is to bring people into relationship, into relationship with God through his son Jesus Christ – to get to know Him.

> Now this is eternal life: that they may know you, the only true God, and Jesus Christ, whom you have sent.[5]

But the aim is also to bring people into relationship with one another. Christ died to restore relationships – relationship with God and relationship with each other – that's what the Cross is about:

> All this is from God, who reconciled us to Himself through Christ and gave us the ministry of reconciliation: that God was reconciling the world to Himself in Christ, not counting people's sins against them. And he has committed to us the message of reconciliation.[6]

My boss (whose sermons I frequently borrow) is fond of pointing out that the very shape of the Cross draws our attention to this double reconciliation. The vertical beam points upwards reminding us of the reconciliation between us and God. The horizontal cross-member reminding us that His death also served to reunite us with our fellow human beings:

> For he Himself is our peace, who has made the two one and has destroyed the barrier, the dividing wall of hostility, by abolishing in his flesh the law with its commandments and

regulations. His purpose was to create in Himself one new person out of the two, thus making peace, and in this one body to reconcile both of them to God through the cross, by which he put to death their hostility.[7]

The ultimate aim of the proclamation of the Good News, the reason for telling people, is to bring them back into relationship. The aim is not just that people's sins are forgiven, rather that sins are forgiven in order that those people can become God's friends once more.

This emphasis on relationship is clearly brought out in John Finney's research. The participants described Christian faith not so much in terms of adhering to certain doctrines, but rather of a friendship to be discovered:

for them the Christian faith is about relationships . . . Nearly all defined a Christian, not so much by what he or she believed, but in terms of friendship and the effect of faith upon their life. It is difficult to overemphasize the importance of this, which is repeated all the way through the survey. Faith is seen in terms of a threeway relationship: with God – with other people – with themselves.[8]

Friendship is at the heart of the Christian faith. If friendship is the aim of the Gospel it is also the prescribed means of spreading the Gospel. Experience of missions in churches of all denominations and all types of churchmanship shows quite clearly it is not the height of churchmanship that determines whether a church will be good at evangelism. Rather it is the depth of relationships that exist in the church. The all-important factor in evangelism is relationship. A church will expand when it has good relations among its members, and when its members have good relationships with outsiders. Halfway through a mission in Torquay the vicar turned to me and said that a worryingly large number of his church had discovered that they had nobody to invite to the evangelistic events in the mission week because the only people they knew were other church members.

Evangelism will not take place unless we have friends to evangelize. And they must be real friends. People will see through a friendship that is motivated only by a desire to convert them. A friend of mine was very keen to attend the Luis Palau Mission when he came to London some years ago. She was rung up and invited by a Christian girl, but turned down the invitation because as she put it, 'This so-called friend only ever gets in touch with me when there is a Christian event which she wants to take me to. The rest of the time she isn't interested.' We have to earn the right to talk about the love of Jesus by showing the love of Jesus. This means we must have time for people. While writing the final draft of this chapter I received a letter from a friend who recently left my community. She wrote:

> I stopped going to church after I realized that my non-Christian friends were more honest with me than my Christian friends were – and that they had more time for me because they had less commitments. Ironic I suppose!

Ironic and tragic. The key to evangelism is relationships, real relationships with real friends. (I shall look at the issue of relationships within a church and the need to build true community in chapter 9.)

In our evangelism training we need therefore to concentrate our energies on enabling ordinary people to reach out the hand of friendship and draw people into relationship not only with themselves, but with the living God. This is the method that God has ordained as the way to spread the message of Christianity. We need to be making friends. That this is the best method should not surprise us, for it is what we find in the Bible. Jesus said, 'As the Father sent me so I send you.'[9] How was Jesus sent? As a human being.[10] In order to communicate His Good News, God had Jesus become human. That was God's method then, and we are asked to continue in that pattern. Human beings, vulnerable human beings, are God's chosen method of spreading the Good News. The reason God chose humans is obvious. Humans are the only 'thing' capable of relationship – capable of relating to people. The Gospel, which is about relating, needs to be shared by those who are capable of relationship. (We shall look at the approach Jesus used in chapter 4; and the need to share ourselves in chapter 6.)

John Finney's research puts the emphasis in evangelism firmly on friendship. It also pulls the rug from underneath most of the common assumptions about the way to do evangelism. Most of our evangelism assumes that people will come to faith suddenly, and our preaching is frequently based on the notion that a crisis will trigger a person's commitment to Christ. But John Finney's research shows that most people do not come to faith as a result of a crisis. More importantly the vast majority of people come to faith gradually. The average length of time taken was four-and-a-half years; the longest took 42 years! We need therefore to explore ways of helping them forward step by step along the road to faith (and I shall explore this theme in chapter 8).

The vast majority of our evangelistic tracts and sermons major on the subject of sin and the opportunity to find forgiveness through Christ and His death on the Cross. But this research shows that sin is seen as irrelevant by most of the people who come to faith. Sin and guilt play very little part in turning people to Christ; only 18% said that a specific guilt helped move them to faith and 49% claimed to feel no guilt at all. If we continue to concentrate so exclusively on this one strand of the Good News in our evangelism then it should come as little surprise that we get such a poor response. (I shall look at the need to broaden our understanding of the Good News in chapters 3, 4 and 5.)

John Finney also puts paid to any suggestion that it is intellectual objections that prevent people coming to faith. Even before becoming Christians only 6% of those in the survey doubted the resurrection and only 3% had difficulty with the Virgin Birth. One of the most inhibiting factors which prevents ordinary Christians talking about their faith is the fear that they will be unable to answer people's objections. It is simply not the case that people are lining up with their intellectual objections ready to shoot down 'us unthought-out Christians'. (I will examine the need to be able to give reasons for our faith and the way to handle difficult questions in chapter 11.)

In evangelism we have a choice. We can carry on as we have been, using methods which for the most part have been shown to be ineffective. Or we can abandon these methods, and the normal presuppositions which go with them, and set off in new and more appropriate ways to spread the Gospel. The latter will involve examining the very content of the Gospel and whether it has any relevance for today. It will mean a long and hard look at ourselves, at our faith, and also our relationships with those outside the circle of faith. But it will be worth it. We will discover that there are ways we can spread the Gospel far more easily and effectively, and with total integrity.

And if we dare to put these discoveries into practice then we will find not only the faith of our friends growing but our own faith being renewed.

DO YOU HAVE ANYTHING
TO DECLARE?

If you travel abroad, on your return you will be confronted not only by Passport Control, but also by Customs. Above the exits for the Customs are two channels – red and green. The red channel is for those people who have goods to declare, whereas you go through the green channel if you have nothing to declare. Sadly there are many dishonest people who try to slip out through the green channel despite the fact that they have goods to declare. I would like to set up green and red channels at the doors of every church in this country. Only instead of saying 'Do you have any goods to declare?' the question would be 'Do you have any Good News to declare?' It strikes me that most Christians are being dishonest and are slipping out of our churches denying the Good News that they carry with them. We must encourage every Christian that they have a duty to own up and to declare the Good News.

Like a customs officer who asks you to open your bags, I want to stop you in your tracks, and invite you to come, to open yourself up for examination to find out just what Good News you are carrying.

Most Christians seem blissfully unaware that they are carrying valuables through the church doors as they leave a service. And unaware that they have a responsibility to share these valuables.

14

EVERY-MEMBER MINISTRY

A modern catch phrase in church circles is 'Every-member ministry'. Every member of a church has a job to do. But the idea is not new. As early as the fourth century St Jerome described Confirmation as the 'ordination of the laity'. Thomas Aquinas taught that at Confirmation the layman was given 'through the Holy Spirit power and responsibility not only to effect his own salvation but also by sharing in the priesthood of Christ to act as His apostle in the salvation of the world'[1]. We are reminded of this in the parting words of the modern Communion service . . .

Go in peace to love and serve the Lord . . . In the name of Christ, Amen.

We are all called to serve the Lord in our daily lives, but what exactly are we expected to do?

We need to look very carefully at the job description Jesus gave his followers because it is His final command. Psychologists will tell you that the most memorable thing in a debate is what is said last. So if you want to influence your audience you must pay close attention to your summing-up speech, the last word is the most important. Christ's command to evangelize comes almost at the end of each of the gospels. The final words somebody says on their death bed, or before departing on a long journey, are likely to be words of import, something to treasure and mull over. Jesus' final words, not on his deathbed, but immediately prior to his ascension into heaven, are words commanding us to evangelize. At the culmination of His earthly ministry Jesus is concerned to encourage His disciples to share the Good News. Let us look at what the four evangelists tell us about that final command, in an endeavour to understand what is meant by evangelism, and just what it is that we are supposed to do.

FIRSTLY, WE ARE TOLD TO 'GO'

In Matthew's account Jesus says to his disciples:

> All authority in heaven and on earth has been given to me. Therefore go and make disciples of all nations . . .[2]

Jesus tells us to 'go', not to sit and wait. We have to go out to meet them and cannot afford to wait for them to come to us. Someone once said 'We were instructed to be fishers of men, not keepers of an aquarium'. We are to be like fishermen, to set out leaving the safety of the shore and actively to cast out our nets. I remember once when I was fishing as young boy a fish jumped out of the sea into our boat. But I wouldn't wait around for it to happen again. We cannot sit comfortably in our churches expecting people to come to us. We need to go out and meet them, leaving the safety and comfort of our church fellowship and venturing into uncharted waters to meet them on their own ground.

Before I start a mission project with a church I often ask them to act out a picture to portray the change that I hope will occur in their church. I ask a dozen people to stand in a circle. Quite naturally they stand in a circle a couple of feet apart, facing inwards. I then comment that this is what most churches look like. Most churches are groups of people who are fairly close but not too close for comfort, and they are looking inwards. Two fundamental changes are needed. First people must get much closer together, their lives should really touch, so I get the group to hold hands. That is the first step to becoming a real church, because now they are really supporting one another. The second change I want to bring about is to turn people inside out! As long as we are facing inwards it is impossible for an outsider to join the circle. If we are to become the Church of Christ we need to be holding hands and supporting one another, but we should be facing outwards, and presenting a welcoming face to outsiders. We need to become inclusive rather than exclusive. So I ask them to turn round and join hands once more. I then point out that Christians are called to step forward in their pilgrimage and ask them what would happen if they did so. Fairly obviously the circle soon gets stretched, and if we are to have people's hands to hold, then we will need new people to join the circle as we step out in faith.

We must turn our churches round so they become outward-looking – after all, the Church has been described as the only club which exists for the sake of its non members.

SECONDLY, WE ARE TOLD THAT WE ARE TO GO TO <u>ALL</u> PEOPLE

Matthew's account of the 'Great Commission' reminds us that disciples are to be made from all nations, a point reinforced in Acts:

> But you will receive power when the Holy Spirit comes on you, and you will be my witnesses in Jerusalem, and in all Judea and Samaria, and to the ends of the earth.[3]

The Good News is for everyone, and is not reserved for a select few. We must be careful to ensure that we are not over possessive about the Good News. We need to be prepared to share it with all and sundry and put up with the consequences of all and sundry joining our church! Woebetide the church that is full of 'people like us', an exclusive club of those we deem acceptable to join our circle. The church must be a hotch-potch of different people who come together despite their different personalities, tastes and life-styles, and who are able to live together because they all belong to one family and love the same father.

THIRDLY, WE ARE TO START WHERE WE ARE

The Good News must be spread to the ends of the earth, but Luke emphasizes that we must start by announcing it in our own back yard. In his gospel Luke makes this clear when he says:

> ... repentance and forgiveness of sins will be preached in His name to all nations **beginning at Jerusalem**.[4]

Yes, the Good News will be preached to all nations, but both the passages in Luke and Acts emphasize that the disciples are to start locally in Jerusalem. The Good News will spread from there, rippling outwards and ultimately travelling round the world. A small stone dropped in a still pool will ultimately create ripples which will spread far and wide. And so it has been with the Christian Faith. This should be profoundly encouraging, making the task of evangelizing the world seem much simpler. The instruction in Luke and Acts means that you and I do not have to go to the ends of the earth. After all if I pass it on to one person and they successfully pass it on to another, then ultimately it will spread round the world. It is rather like the carrying of the Olympic Flame from one venue to the next. Like the Olympic runner we have the responsibility simply to play our part in the relay that will see the light of Christ carried right around the world.

Equally the instruction to start at home, in Jerusalem or wherever you are, is a reminder that evangelism is not about talking to strangers, but far more about telling neighbours and friends whom we already know and who live locally. I often surprise people who come to Lee Abbey, by saying to them 'never evangelize a stranger'. I say it to be deliberately provocative and not to deny that once in a blue moon people get converted by meeting total strangers in a train and getting into conversation. But it makes the point that we have enough friends to evangelize without any need to go any further and it is these people, our friends, that all too often we ignore when thinking about evangelism. When I first mention the word mission nearly always church people will ask me whether they are going to be required to do door-knocking. People seem to have defined evangelism as approaching strangers and it is not surprising that we feel uncomfortable about doing so. But far from approaching strangers, Jesus' instruction in Luke and Acts reminds us to start with those closer to home.

FOURTHLY, OUR ROLE IS TO BE 'WITNESSES'

The word Jesus uses to define the disciples' role is 'witness':

Then he opened their minds so they could understand the

Scriptures. He told them, 'This is what is written: The Christ will suffer and rise from the dead on the third day, and repentance and forgiveness of sins will be preached in his name to all nations, beginning at Jerusalem. You are witnesses of these things. I am going to send you what my Father has promised; but stay in the city until you have been clothed with power from on high.'[5]

The job description given to the disciples is to be 'witnesses'. The term witness has become standard terminology in some Christian circles. So much so that it has become jargon – with typically bad grammatical sense people talk about witnessing or say 'I witnessed' for my faith. Other legal terminology such as the word testimony is also used in certain Christian circles. Despite familiarity with the word, all too often the association and meaning have got lost. 'Witness' has become a jargon word divorced from its roots and meaning. The word witness obviously comes from a legal, courtroom context. A witness is called to testify. Several important points should be made. First, we are not called to be prosecution or defence counsel. It is not our job to argue the case. We don't have to try and persuade people or put the case across as a witness. It is not the job of the witness to try and persuade the judge or jury in any particular direction, that is the job of the barrister or solicitor. Rather it is the job of a witness to describe what he or she has experienced.

I have a summons from the West Midlands Police. No, I haven't done anything wrong, I have simply been summoned to be a witness in a case about dangerous driving. The case concerns an incident one Friday morning on the M6 northbound carriageway between junctions 8 & 9. West Midlands Police sent me a five-page questionnaire to fill in. After some preliminary questions about name, age etc., the crunch question is No. 8. It says in bold, **'describe in your own words exactly how the accident happened'.** (Note in passing that it emphasises **in your own words.** Christians all too often have a desperate problem with jargon which they have borrowed from other people and whose meaning has become lost in the borrowing.) Then in bold letters the questionnaire carries on and says, in letters double sized, as well as bold, **'STATE ONLY WHAT YOU SAW OR HEARD YOURSELF'.** They are only interested in what you have experienced personally. Similarly when it comes to evangelism the key thing that is going to be of interest to other people is what you personally have experienced of Jesus Christ: The difference he has made to you – the answers to prayer you have received. You cannot be a witness on behalf of somebody else or somebody else's experience.

I remember on one of our missions talking to the vicar's wife after she had attended a coffee morning for young mums, where some of our team had spoken about their faith. 'How did it go?' I asked. 'Fine for the most part.' I could tell she wasn't totally happy but that she felt embarrassed about being critical. 'Come on,' I said, 'tell me what you didn't like about it. Did something go wrong?' 'Well not exactly,' she said. 'For most of the time it was great, the team were talking about their experience and the mums were really listening. But then one of the team started talking about Jackie Pullinger's work in Hong Kong and how drug addicts are being healed of their drug dependency. You could see the women turning off. It just didn't cut any ice with them.' I knew exactly what she meant, and I knew why the person had been tempted to switch the conversation to talk about Jackie Pullinger. Very often our own stories, our testimonies about what God has done in our lives, seem

21

very humdrum, very mundane and even a little boring. People often say to me, 'But my conversion isn't spectacular, there is nothing worth sharing.' How wrong they are. It doesn't need to be spectacular to be worth sharing. Most people's lives are not dramatic, they are by definition, ordinary. Most of the people with whom we are called to talk about our faith are ordinary people leading ordinary lives. And it is our ordinary testimonies of how God has affected us very ordinary people that will mean most, and make most connection, with these people. The mistake the girl made in switching the conversation away from the ordinary personal stories to talking about the spectacular deeds of Jackie Pullinger was that she was passing on something second-hand – it was not something she had witnessed herself and therefore seemed remote to the audience.

This feeling that our story is not spectacular enough to be worth telling is very common. When I ask people if they mind me interviewing them about their Christian journey, I nearly always get the response: 'There is nothing very much to tell – there was nothing dramatic about my conversion.' I always reply that I am not only interested in your conversion but in all of your Christian journey and secondly, I am not looking for anything dramatic, I am looking to tell the truth.

Sadly, many Christians do not apply the requirements placed on a witness in a court of law, when it comes to being a witness for Christ. If you stand in a court of law in the witness box, you place one hand on the Bible and you are required to swear:

I swear to tell the truth, the whole truth and nothing but the truth.

When it comes to giving our Christian testimony we need to

apply this dictum. We have no permission to embellish, to add, or to withhold anything. We are required to tell people exactly what we have experienced of the risen Lord Jesus. Not to add to it in an attempt to make it sound better, and not to hold anything back. It is the whole truth that is required, not an edited or doctored version.

FIFTHLY, WE ARE PROMISED HELP TO FULFIL THE TASK

Luke stresses that the disciples will be given help to fulfil their task. In Acts we are told: 'You will receive power when the Holy Spirit comes on you.'[6] And in the gospel of Luke the disciples are urged to wait and not act until 'they have been clothed with power from on high'.[7] As I shook hands with the congregation following my first ever service at St Giles', where I was the brand new curate, the oldest member of the congregation, a lady called Winifred who was in her nineties, placed into my hands a bookmark. On it are written the words 'The will of God will never lead you where the grace of God cannot keep you'. It was a tremendous encouragement to a very nervous and over-awed curate, just setting out on his ministry, to be reminded that God's grace is sufficient to enable us to do all that he has called us to do. And this is what Jesus is promising. We are not being asked to do it in our own strength but clothed with power from on high. He will do it through us. The Holy Spirit will prompt us and remind us.[8] The Holy Spirit will be testifying and so must we.[9] The Holy Spirit will work inside people's conscience so that they become aware of their spiritual condition.[10] And He will guide us to speak the truth.[11] We are not alone in this task. God is with us through His Holy Spirit, and

Luke and Acts remind us that we are not to try doing it on our own but must lean on and wait for the help of the Holy Spirit.

The final sentence in Matthew's gospel contains Jesus' promise of help:

> And surely I am with you always, to the very end of the age.[12]

This sentence can help us enormously as we face the daunting task of evangelism. It reminds us that we are not alone, that we are not required to do it in our own strength but that Jesus will help us.

Also, and more profoundly, it reminds us that Jesus is with us and therefore people can meet Jesus when they meet us. I am always encouraging people involved in evangelism not to forget that God is there meeting people and that it is not all up to us. Whenever we go out on our missions we usually fall into the same trap of thinking 'It's all up to us'. We need to remind ourselves that actually Jesus is there too and really it is all up to Him. This is just as well since often we cannot manage on our own – as I found out with my mother, but I'll leave her story to the next chapter.

HONEY, I SHRUNK THE GOSPEL

There is an old adage that says, 'I hear – I forget; I see – I remember; I do – I understand.' Perhaps a fourth line should be added: 'I fail – I change my approach.' It is through reflecting on my failures in evangelism that I have learnt most, and in the hope that others too may learn I give below an account of one such failure.

For a number of years following my own conversion aged 22 I worked on converting my mother. With good evangelistic zeal I took every opportunity when visiting her to talk about faith. This was welcomed by my mother who was genuinely interested in discovering what gripped her son. Luckily we have a relationship that could withstand the verbal battering I gave her from the rather narrow and bigoted position I then held.

Our discussions centred around the role of Jesus. Early in our conversation I remember her telling me that although she had a belief in God, she found it difficult to see how to relate to Jesus. She couldn't see where He fitted into the picture. As a newly converted evangelical I thought I knew what to do. I totally ignored her belief in God (whereas now I see I should have begun by teasing this out), and set to work on explaining the role of Jesus. I was going to a good evangelical church where I was receiving 'sound' teaching. And this I passed on to my mother, convinced that if only she could understand the role played by Jesus then soon inevitably she would get converted. I told her all about the incarnation; that Jesus is God come down to earth. I told her why He came – to die. And then I told her why He died. I gave her the classic (evangelical) presentation of the Gospel.

Did she get converted? No. So what did I do? It may sound moronic but for two years I simply repeated it. Over and over again I went on and on, like a record stuck in a groove, about Jesus dying to save her from her sins. It was all the Good News I knew how to share. Visit after visit we talked, amicably, but it made no difference. I constantly wondered at my mother's stupidity in being unable to grasp the significance of Jesus. My lengthy, and accurate, theological explanations made no impression on my mother. She made no step forward in her faith.

Until one day when it all changed. She rang me up. She'd had a dream 'and now I understand about Jesus' she told me, and summoned me round to hear about her dream. I jumped straight into the car, hared round, and she told me what had happened. Jesus had appeared to her in a dream, dressed in flowing robes (as He would to my mother since she is quite traditional). He'd spoken to her and now she understood. 'Come on, what did He say?' I demanded. 'He said "think of me as a friend" ' she replied. 'Oh no,' I thought, 'how banal. Little difference that is going to make.' I was terribly disappointed.

But I was wrong. That sentence transformed her life. From that point on her faith leapt forward. She began to pray daily, until soon she found that if pressure of work on the farm caused her to miss her morning prayers then she simply had to stop and make time later. Far from being banal, that simple sentence contained the Good News she needed to hear. She didn't need to hear about her sins being forgiven. What she first of all needed to hear was that Jesus was her friend.

So where did I go wrong? In all that two-year period, I had made two crucial mistakes. First of all I did not discover till much later that it would not be a true description of my mother to say she was faithless. How many people could we really describe as having no faith at all? Rather my mother had a very profound faith in God that had for 30 years or so lain dormant. Indeed she had an 'evangelical' faith in as much as she made a 'commitment' to God when she was seventeen. What subsequently happened in her life, marriage to my father and having four children, effectively served to push God into a very secondary place. What needed to happen, therefore, was not her conversion but rather the rekindling of the faith that throughout all those years had remained, but which had dwindled until it had become only softly glowing embers.

The second mistake I made was to narrow down the Good News. For I had been taught an unnatural and ineffective technique which inhibited me from capitalizing on my greatest asset, my own story of what excited me about Jesus. I knew exactly which thread of the Good News attracted me, that set my heart on fire and made me first follow the Christian faith and commit myself to Christ. And it was not the fact that Jesus died to save me from my sins. My first real step forward in faith, that made me resolve to follow Jesus, was concerned not so much with the death of Christ but with His rising. My own conversion happened in a logical way, when I read a book my then girlfriend lent me – a book which incidentally she had not read. It was John Stott's *Basic Christianity*. The evidence he put forward convinced me that the Resurrection had taken place. That was the first vital ingredient in bringing me to faith. The second crucial part took place in a graveyard one sunny morning. A Christian friend of mine was talking to a non-Christian girl. Eventually, worn down by the evidence for the Resurrection, she took another tack in order to get off the hook. 'OK', she said, 'supposing I'm convinced that the Resurrection did take place, so what? It is an awful long time ago. What difference does it make to me?' His reply was blunt and rude. 'You really don't see what difference His rising again makes to you? Then you're thick.' The girl was offended, but quickly replied, 'Come on then, wise guy, tell me!' I listened fascinated, for I could not answer the question either. 'Don't you see?' he went on. 'If He died and came back to life, then obviously He is more powerful than death, and death cannot hold Him down. So He must still be alive today.' As he spoke those last words a soft wave washed over me and I experienced an incredible stillness. A truth had dawned on me. I remember nothing more of the conversation, nor what happened to the girl. What happened to me was I had been grabbed hold of by a truth so simple, so obvious and yet so profound: Jesus had died and risen again, which meant He was still around . . . Which meant I could find Him. That thought thrilled and excited me. It was this fact, the fact that I might be able to get to know this extraordinary, powerful God, that grabbed my imagination.

The Good News about the Cross and forgiveness of sins only got through to me later, though I knew it in my head in a cold, aloof way. I felt guilty and troubled, and thought my faith inadequate if not verging on the heretical. It is these feelings of guilt that we must counteract in order to liberate people to share 'their' Good News. Ministers must stop telling congregations what the Good News of Jesus is, and instead allow them to tell their stories. It may not fit a neatly packaged version of the Good News, but I believe it will let loose a new and powerful proclamation of the Gospel. We must, however, realize that though one particular aspect of the Gospel excited us, the person to whom we are talking may be quite different. It may simply leave them cold. This is one reason that the Church is called to evangelize corporately, since in the Church the full breadth of the Good News should be contained, ready to meet the need of the outsider. For we need to carry with us far more than the truth that led to our conversion, we need to be able to share what we have learnt since; and the exciting things we have seen in others in our church.

Whenever I teach at Lee Abbey on this subject of evangelism, I encourage people to do something very simple in order to broaden their understanding of the content of the Gospel. Whenever they read the Bible (daily I hope) I encourage them to ask themselves a simple question: 'What aspect of the Good News is contained in this passage of Scripture?' If reading John, it might be about love; if Hebrews, it might be about heaven; if Jeremiah, it might be about hope in times of desperation, and so on. Thus our daily Bible reading should have a direct effect on our praise and worship and also on our ability to evangelize. For we need to take every opportunity to rediscover the breadth of the Good News of Jesus Christ.

A friend of mine once asked a car dealer whether he enjoyed being a salesman. The man paused, then admitted that, in fact, he hated every single minute of it. It was not that he disliked being a salesman as such. Indeed, he made it clear that there were times in his career when he enjoyed it. What the salesman hated was that presently he had no confidence in the product he was required to sell. Day after day he was called to be enthusiastic about something he did not and could not believe in. He longed to sell something he could genuinely enthuse about.

Now I do not wish to suggest that spreading the Gospel is akin to selling cars, or indeed to selling anything. But in many Christians' experience there seems to be something akin to what our sad car salesman felt. Many Christians are not enthusiastic about evangelism because they are not enthusiastic about the Good News.

Now sometimes the problem lies in the individual. They need to become enthusiastic about the 'product', to fall in love with Jesus. But very often the fault lies with the Good News itself. The Gospel we are asked to 'sell' is not exciting, and does not excite them and we can only spread with lacklustre conviction what has only partially excited us.

It's not that the Good News of Jesus really is dull, but the aspect of the Good News of Jesus that we tend to express frequently is. There is a huge gulf between the Good News that God would want His world to hear and the Good News that we are telling others. The awful truth is that we have distorted the Good News. The version of the Gospel we are communicating tends to be limp and childishly inadequate, and we are rightly ashamed of it. It is time to share the more taxing version of the Good News that enlivens the pages of the Bible.

Oddly enough many Christians do sense that there is something wrong with the Good News they are telling others, but they're not sure what. I am sure this is one reason why so many mature Christians continue to ask evangelists the same old question: 'Can you please give me the Gospel in a nutshell?' But ironically, what evangelists have done in response to the request for a simple Gospel outline has actually been disastrous for the proclamation of the Gospel. In an attempt to help the ordinary Christian, we have produced an array of simple aids, such as tracts explaining how to become a Christian in words and pictures, or even a minimalist version with four key

Bible verses. Well motivated as the idea is, the side effect has
been devastating.

A recent film was entitled 'Honey, I shrunk the kids'. The
same could be said for much of the current teaching on evangelism – we have shrunk the Gospel. And as a result we are left
with something that is skimpy and inadequate. It just doesn't
fit the bill – it doesn't cover the everyday situations of most
people today.

I am not suggesting that we need to invent a new Gospel for
our age; the Good News is unchanging. What I am arguing is
that in our generation we have belittled it, shrunk it almost
beyond recognition, by concentrating on a so-called 'core
Gospel outline'. It is time for a rediscovery of the richness of
the Gospel, that will once again take us back to its roots in the
Bible and the life and work of Jesus.

If the Christian evangelist reduces the vast mystery of faith
to a few lines that might come off a corn flake packet, or
offers slick moral answers as if they can be drawn out of a
machine, he is dealing in cartoons, not masterpieces, and
sowing cynicism and derision rather than faith . . .

The temptation to reduce Christian truths to Christmas
cracker phrases is often well intentioned, but we should not
be surprised if it ends in provoking uneasiness and contempt. The temptation to offer processed food, slick
answers, easy sentimentalities, slogans and jingles, as repre-
senting the mind and heart of Almighty God and the awesome mysteries of salvation, may be powerful in an
increasingly shallow culture, but there comes a point when
even the laziest consumers begin to realise it damages the
health . . . Better for people to shrink from the Gospel
because it is too great than because it is too small.[1]

Rebecca Manley Pippert in her superb book on evangelism entitled *Out of the Saltshaker* refers to a tragic example of how we have reduced the Gospel down to cartoon proportions:

> I remember being with a Christian student on a beach. Bob and I met several non-Christians and began talking about all sorts of things. Eventually the conversation got around to Christianity, and it was a lively and invigorating discussion. We even exchanged addresses before leaving. I was feeling very good about the conversation, but Bob seemed very quiet. When I asked him what was wrong he said: 'I thought it was an absolute failure. There are four major points to the Gospel and you only brought in two of them, and they weren't even in the right order.' . . . I stared at him in disbelief and sadness. Here was a young man who genuinely loved God . . . And yet he had missed the entire point. He was sure his agenda, his four points, were the supreme value. Yet his programme was so rigid that real-life human beings could not penetrate it.[2]

Frequently on missions I see Christians who out of nervousness arm themselves with a formulaic summary of the Gospel which they then fire off at every opportunity. And then they are surprised that it has little effect, or go even further and place the blame not on the inappropriateness of their 'technique', but on the hardness of the heart of the listener. What they have failed to see is that the Good News that they are attempting to communicate is making no impression on their audience because it makes no connection with where that person 'is at'. It does not connect with their real life. Making a formula of the Gospel dehumanizes it. The Gospel is personal. God speaks to individuals. So God's message to humans cannot be reduced to a video or booklet that can be brought out for every occasion. Surely individuals are needed to share the Gospel because only individuals are able to respond to the infinite variety that they will find when they meet other people. When we make the Gospel into a standard package it prevents us bringing out our own particular story, and the thread of Good News that has excited us. It also depersonalizes the person with whom we are talking. Instead of responding to their uniqueness we simply thrust the same package at them. Think of the care and thought that goes into selecting appropriate presents for your friends and family at Christmas. You wouldn't dream of giving everyone exactly the same gift – the same applies with giving away the Gospel, choose appropriate 'Good News' for each friend.

The traditional teaching on the practise of evangelism has tended to brainwash Christians by dulling their appreciation of the Good News. Teaching people a formula can eventually make them forget or dismiss as unimportant what it was that actually converted them. For years my wife felt inadequate, or even at times was made to doubt she was a Christian, because her church taught the magic formula that a converted Christian is someone who becomes aware of their sins, repents and believes in the forgiveness won by Christ on the Cross. In my wife's case that awareness and repentance of sins did not come until some years after her conversion, a conversion brought about by seeing that only with Jesus Christ in control of her life could her full potential be achieved. On a variety of definitions of a 'Christian' my wife had passed the test well before she had confessed her sinfulness in any meaningful way. If we define a Christian as someone for whom Jesus is Lord, He was Lord even before she became aware of sin. If we say it is someone who follows Jesus then she was on the Christian journey even before she left her sin at the Cross. If we say a Christian is someone who invites Jesus to come into their heart (based on the picture of Revelation 3:20) then she had truly and very meaningfully done so.

We need to realize that a Christian is someone who responds to the Good News by making Christ the centre of their life. And we must realize, too, that that which induces someone to take that monumental step is not always the news that our sins are forgiven. There are many other reasons for people being persuaded to place their life in Jesus' hands.

This is not a new idea. As long ago as 1945 a report of the Church of England Commission entitled *Towards the Conversion of England*, defined the Christian life as not necessarily dependent on whether or not a person had repented of their sins:

Conversion is the reorientation of life from self to God through Christ Jesus.[3]

And they expressed the idea that different people responded to different aspects of the Good News when they went on to say:

The act of conversion is the personal acceptance of Christ Jesus as Saviour and King. In the Retrospect of his life Bishop Hensley Henson recalls how he asked Bishop Linton, 'the most successful evangelist of Moslems that our church possesses . . . what he found appealed most to the Mohammedans in Persia.' The answer was that 'it was the Person and Character of Christ *NOT* conviction of sin. The sense of sin developed in converts, but it played no part in their conversion.' Bishop Linton finds the same equally true in Birmingham.[4]

We must be prepared to accept that the steps of the Christian pilgrimage vary, and they do not always occur in the same order for each individual. And most importantly we must enable Christians to share their different routes to faith, to emphasize different dimensions of the Good News, and not to feel guilty if they don't mention sin or the Cross. We cannot expect someone who is grabbed by the fact of Jesus giving them a purpose in life, to major on talking about Heaven. And we must not ask someone whose faith was born out of a sense of belonging, to say that the Good News is that his sins have been forgiven.

But we have also been in danger of going a stage further and reducing our understanding of the Gospel until it is almost content-less. Recently on a mission at a church I was told: 'The drama group really want to hit people with the Gospel.' When it came to the end of the week I was really disappointed at what the drama group contributed – not because the acting was poor, but because the content of the scripts was so empty. Each and every drama contained at its core the same message; a threat of what happened should you fail to respond. But they did not contain any content about what it was you were to respond to. The drama group had said that they wanted to hit people with the Good News, but there was no Good News contained in any of the dramas. By the end of the week I was left wondering if they knew any Good News, or whether a lack of Good News in the sketches reflected a lack of Good News in their theology.

I often wonder whether the same was true of the famed Victorian 'Hell-Fire and Judgement' preaching. Had they forgotten what Good News there was? When we emphasize the negative I fear it may reflect that we lack something positive to preach. While I believe we should preach on such themes as judgement and hell, and have done so myself, I do not believe they can ever be the mainstay of evangelistic endeavour. For we are commanded to go out and preach *Good* News, not to go out and harangue with threats. Perhaps our clergy should be challenged to give a series of twenty sermons, all of them positive, which focus on different aspects of the Good News of Jesus. Then we might see how many of our preachers dry up, and find out how much of a message we actually have to offer!

The Gospel has been reduced to a caricature, so we must reverse this process and ensure that it is reduced no further. We must get people to rip up their cartoon line drawings and hand them a full palette of colours. And then we must teach them once again how to paint pictures of God that have the power of masterpieces. What is needed is a reawakening to the mystery and depth of the Good News.

The Good News is like a carpet – a Persian carpet. But we have made it into a monochrome rug. The Good News itself is richly coloured and varied, made up of different themes like the different coloured threads of the rug, each combining to make up the beautiful and exquisite pattern that is portrayed by the different writers of the Bible. Instead of a neatly ordered systematic presentation of theology, the Bible is a hugely varied tapestry or carpet. That the Bible is made up of a collection of different themes should hardly surprise us; it is after all more of a library than a single book. To change the analogy, the Bible is like a huge orchestral score, with each of the writers playing a particular instrument. Some may be louder and more to the fore than others, but it is the harmony of all the different voices or instruments playing together that makes for the great masterpiece. In any great orchestral work there are a number of themes and different movements, with the themes being echoed and voiced by the different players, developing, expanding and repeating the central theme of the composer. Likewise, the Good News is made up of a myriad number of themes which combine and harmonize in the portrayal of the great theme.

Reading through the Gospels we can identify these multiple threads woven together by the evangelists. Different people will be drawn into faith by the different threads. I am not simply suggesting that we need to be sensitive to people's varied personalities and to approach them in appropriate ways, but of course this is essential. Rather I am also suggesting that we need to approach different people with different parts of the Good News, and the content of the Good News we share should be appropriate to each person we meet. The content of the Good News, as well as the styling of presentation, should be tailor-made to suit each individual. I am no fisherman, but the bait used to lure fish will vary according to what type of fish you are trying to catch. Similarly with people, to urge them into the 'keep-net' of the Church will require that the bait used is palatable. The Good News will be different for different people. The truth of this can be seen quite plainly in the New Testament in the way that Jesus approaches different people and uses different angles of the Good News to draw them into relationship. Jesus should be a model for our evangelism, so let us look at Jesus' approach.

4

HOW DID JESUS DO IT?

Jesus was Good News incarnate. He embodied the Good News, and everyone He met in one sense encountered Good News as being part of the beauty of God in Jesus Christ. The Good News was shown in His character, His personality – His every action demonstrated it. But as well as showing people Good News, Jesus also proclaimed it. He spoke Good News to everyone He met. But the Good News was different for different people. Jesus chose a different coloured thread according to the personality of the person He was addressing. A different theme from the Good News was used by Jesus as His starting point for each of His different conversations. He selected that theme with great care, applying the particular strand of Good News which that person needed to hear.

Jesus should be our model for evangelism. So we shall look at four incidents from the gospels to discover some of the different aspects of the Good News that Jesus gave to the different people in each story. As we look at these four incidents not only will we see the principle of applying different Good News to different people, but at the same time we will be expanding our understanding of the Good News.

A. LUKE 17: 11-14: TEN MEN SUFFERING FROM LEPROSY

Ten men, suffering from leprosy, came to meet Jesus. Stopping some way off they called out to Him: 'Jesus, master, take pity on us.' What Good News did Jesus have for these men? The Good News for the ten lepers may not be immediately obvious to us at first, but is contained in Jesus' words to them, when He says: 'Go and show yourselves to the priests.' To understand the Good News, we need to understand the context. The ten lepers were outcasts, expelled and excluded from the community by their illness. That is why they didn't come right up to Jesus, but addressed Him from some distance. In those days there was no National Health Service. They didn't go to the local general practitioner for a sick note. Instead the priest performed that function. It was the job of the priest to carry out examinations and declare whether a person was sick or whether he was well. The statement by Jesus 'Go and show yourselves to the priests' therefore means two things. Firstly, I will heal you and secondly, because you are healed, you can once again join the community, so go to the priest and perform the necessary checks set out in Leviticus 14. In His approach to these men then, Jesus doesn't mention sin or forgiveness of sins. Rather, the theme of Good News He uses concerns healing, acceptance and inclusion back into the community. It is indeed all Good News for the lepers, all of whom are healed, as Jesus points out when only one returns.

The Good News that Jesus gave to the lepers is highly applicable today. Without suggesting that you will meet any lepers on your daily travels in suburbia, you will certainly come across outcasts. Think through the different categories of people who represent today's lepers: drunks; the homeless; travellers or gypsies; all of them excluded from normal society. It is little wonder that Mother Teresa's actions in caring for these types of people speak so powerfully of the God of love who welcomes and embraces the destitute and lonely. Likewise the work of the Salvation Army and other organizations in reaching out to include these people and offer practical support. We opened our church hall one Christmas to welcome the homeless, with teams of church members to provide not only food and clothing but also conversation. Just being with them demonstrated to them in this small way that they remained a part of our society and our community. Evangelism must be by deed as well as by word.

There are other groups who can feel equally outcast. Single parents, whether divorcees, widows or the unmarried can in middle-class culture feel terribly isolated and excluded. After all, no one wants to invite an attractive divorcee to a dinner party. It makes for odd numbers, and there is an undercurrent of fear that maybe she or he will lure away someone else's partner. When couples separate often the only friends they have are mutual friends, which can make for a great deal of awkwardness and can in turn lead to one person being 'dropped' out of embarrassment. We must seek to include these modern outcasts, keep them on as our friends. We must work against their becoming estranged from society.

Perhaps the most obvious group of outcasts is those suffering from the AIDS virus. They really are the modern lepers. The fear of catching the disease, its newness, ignorance, and the social stigma that goes with the implications of homosexuality or promiscuity, all conspire to make the person suffering from AIDS an outcast. Unlike someone dying of cancer, an AIDS sufferer often cannot talk about or admit the disease to his closest friends. The Good News I would want to bring to an

AIDS patient is 'you are not an outcast, you are not excluded from my society, nor from God's'. It is this thread of Good News that strikes me as peculiarly relevant, a thread powerfully portrayed several years ago when Princess Diana was filmed holding hands with someone suffering from AIDS. In Indian culture the lowest caste are called literally, 'The Untouchables'. Princess Diana's action spoke volumes of good news, declaring to the world that AIDS patients are not untouchables. She reached into their world and in that touch drew them back into the community. So did Jesus. So must we.

B. JOHN 8 3–11: THE WOMAN CAUGHT IN ADULTERY

Here is a story in which sinfulness is self-evident. The woman has been caught red-handed but Jesus has Good News for her. There are several threads that we can unravel from the text. Firstly, Jesus refuses to condemn her. He is explicitly asked to do so and challenged to apply the law of Moses by the people who brought the woman in front of Him. Whatever the enigmatic writing in the sand may mean, His silence is indicative of His refusal. The second thread of Good News for the woman comes indirectly in His statement to her accusers: 'Let the one among you who is guiltless be the first to throw a stone at her.' The bad news for them is Good News for her. Jesus declared that they are no different from the woman, all of them are sinners and she is no worse. With her particular sin exposed for all the world to see, she must have felt utterly alone and uniquely guilty. But in challenging them in this way, Jesus is pointing out that although she is a sinner, she is no different from all the rest. For we are all sinners.

41

Then Jesus addresses two statements to the woman which contain Good News. He explicitly states that He doesn't condemn her, she is forgiven. And then He says, 'Go away and from this moment sin no more.' The Good News in that last statement is that she can break the habit, she can change the pattern of sinning, she can cease her adultery. The Good News is hope. She can lead a different life from now on. It is a fresh start, a new beginning, with no condemnation and a future ahead of her.

Modern-day parallels with the woman caught in adultery may not be so far below the surface. Although adultery is increasingly common, particularly among men, it does not mean there is no sense of guilt accompanying it. Research by *Cosmopolitan* magazine some years ago showed that many men after committing adultery are actually physically sick. Perhaps their bodies are reflecting something of their inner feelings about themselves and their actions. We need to bring Good News to those caught in the web of adultery. Perhaps to those close friends of ours who commit adultery we need to give both of the statements that Jesus addressed to the women. Sharing the compassion in His 'I don't condemn you', but also the challenge of, 'Don't carry on with this'.

But there is a far wider group of people than simply today's adulterers who need to hear the Good News that Jesus gave to the woman. Many people I meet have a picture of God as a stern, vicious Victorian father, ready to lash out and punish any mistake we make. If our pictures of God the Father are built on our experiences of our earthly fathers, then perhaps it is little surprise that so many people imagine a vindictive God. My grandfather actually had a whip on the table. If my own father or his brother should make the slightest error in manners, an elbow coming too near to the table, the whip would lash out.

The idea of a God who is out to get me, who is eagerly waiting for the smallest mistake, and who will come down on it like a ton of bricks, is very prevalent today. To people who hold this picture of God we must bring the Good News that Jesus gave to the woman: 'God is not out to condemn you.' We must tell them that far from coming to catch them out, God came to show His love and acceptance. We must speak Jesus' words: 'The Son of Man came not to judge but to save'.[1] We must speak to people of the God of Love, who loved so much that He was prepared to give over His only Son in order to win us back and to give us back life. A God that would do anything to give us back freedom. We must give them the Good News that their picture of God is wrong, a gross distortion of the God of Love. And we must help them replace it with a picture of the God who is as beautiful as Jesus.

At the time of the Gulf War I remember reading an account in the *Observer* newspaper of a tank battle that had taken place during the Second World War. It described in gruesome detail the horror of warfare, and how the British unit had returned to the battle site on the following day to witness a scene of total carnage. The author, a tank driver, ended the article with this sentence: 'I know that my soul will be damned in hell for all time because of what I did that day.' That man is all too well aware of sin and guilt. The words that he needs to hear are the same that Jesus spoke to the woman: 'I do not condemn you'. The glorious news of forgiveness may be hard for some people to believe, nevertheless it is this truth about the forgiveness of sins that we must announce.

It is important for those of us who have been taught in evangelical circles to remember two truths concerning sin and the proclamation of the Gospel. Firstly, as I have tried to show above, sin is not necessarily the correct starting point for the proclamation of the Good News. Secondly, on the occasions when sin is the relevant issue, the Good News always concerns *forgiveness* of sins. It may sound strange but in our enthusiasm to deal with the issue of sin in a generation that is largely unconscious of it, we often make the mistake of speaking about sin without mentioning the Good News that it is forgiven. Vincent Donovan, a Roman Catholic priest who became a missionary in East Africa, made this mistake in his evangelization of the Masai. While trying to communicate about the consciousness and reality of sin he was asked by one of the Masai, 'Can you people bring forgiveness of sin?' In his ignorance he ignored it as a stupid question and reverted to trying to raise an awareness of sin in the Masai. Only later did he realize that they were fully aware of sin. What they knew nothing about was its forgiveness. Studying the New Testament approach to evangelization Donovan concluded:

If you study the apostolic approach very closely, you will see that something is missing. Sin is missing. There is no mention of original sin or of any other kind of sin. Sin will come in later, after Christ, after getting to know Christ, in relation to Christ, but the sin portrayed by the first preachers of the Christian Gospel is forgiven sin, something entirely different – the *felix culpa*. After all, isn't that the only kind of sin there is in the world, forgiven sin?[2]

But it is not only in apostolic preaching, it is in the teaching of Jesus himself:

Christ after his resurrection said the same thing: 'Now that the resurrection is a reality, now that forgiveness of sins is accomplished in this new covenant, go out to all the earth and preach the Good News of the forgiveness of sins to all the nations.' Isn't that what he is recorded as saying in Luke and elsewhere?[3]

C. MARK 10: 17–22: THE RICH MAN

Whenever I do this exercise with people, asking them to find the Good News that Jesus gives in each of the different incidents, it is with this story of the rich man that people have the most difficulty. For some reason most people fail to see Good News in the story. They look up at me blankly halfway through the exercise, or say 'But it is bad news for the rich man surely?' No, Jesus gave the rich man Good News. Let's look at the story more closely. The rich man approaches Jesus and says, 'Good master, what must I do to inherit eternal life?' Put more crudely, the man wants to go to heaven and he wants to know how to get there. Indeed, he wants it so badly that he has aspired to keep the law rigorously all his life, and when he says so to Jesus, Jesus' response is one of love. Then comes the Good News. Paraphrasing it, Jesus' reply says, 'You can have what you long for. And I will tell you how to get it. Sell you what you possess, give it away, follow me and it is yours.' This is very Good News. Certainly the man is sad because there is a cost, but the price is worth paying. Indeed, Jesus' use of the phrase 'treasure in heaven' is like saying 'what you want is so valuable it is worth giving up everything for', the same point He brings out in the parable of the pearl of great price. Note once again that the Good News Jesus gives to this man does not mention sin nor its forgiveness. Rather the thread of Good News for the rich man is about heaven, the route to heaven and the price to be paid to get there.

45

The Good News that Jesus gave to the rich man is all too applicable in Western Europe in the twentieth century, in a culture founded on consumerism and materialistic values. The accumulation of wealth has become a god in its own right, and yet it is clearly a god that fails to satisfy the longings of the human heart. Possessions do not answer the deepest needs of people. I remember watching the removal of the Berlin Wall in 1989, and in effect witnessing the end of communism. A learned friend of mine said to me, 'We have seen communism abandoned for failing to fulfil the needs of people. How much longer will it be before we similarly abandon consumerism?' Mike Starkey in his very perceptive analysis of our culture entitled *Born to Shop*, shows up the emptiness of our 'Loadsa-money Culture';

> Into the vacuum left by debunked myths and scorned ideals came consumerism, calling on us to find our identity in purchases, fashions and screen idols. It told us we were truly free if we could choose between a panoply of goodies on megastore shelves. We could find happiness through material things. Greed was the creed; profit, efficiency and pleasure the yardsticks we used to measure what was successful or desirable. The most intense one-minute experience available to modern mankind is that won in a local newspaper quiz where a person is given a minute to rush round a local store in a mad rush of adrenalin and throw all they can into a trolley.[4]

The Good News is that there is more to life. Heaven is for real and contains far more treasure than you can cram into any trolley, more than you can possibly dream of, and it can begin now. Eternal life, life lived in a profoundly fulfilling, rather than superficially satisfying way, is here for the asking, and Jesus shows us it.

Numbers of my wealthiest friends need to hear this thread of the Good News. I want to make them pause and consider whether their headlong pursuit of wealth is achieving anything other than an ulcerated stomach, an estranged family, and the chance of early cardiac arrest. Too many of my friends leave their beautiful homes at six-thirty in the morning, returning at nine-thirty at night, five days a week, with work brought home to do on the weekend. Indeed this has become so normal in some places of work that to stand out against it is to run the risk of being sacked. It happened to one of my parishioners who was called in to see his boss and 'invited' to do a fourteen-hour day. It would have meant that he never saw his wife or his children all week. Six months after refusing, his firm took the earliest opportunity that came along to make him redundant.

Too many people get caught on the materialistic merry-go-round and I fear that some will never get off until they retire, unless they fall off. They are throwing their lives away on hollow dreams. It is a vicious circle; I need more money to buy the things which will bring me and my family happiness, so I must work longer and harder in order to get the money. In the end you work so long and hard that you never get to see your family.

The Good News is that there is another way to live. It may require drastic action, like giving up some materialism to rediscover things that are more important. Like the rich man in the story, the cost of change might seem too high. But in the end perhaps it is a small price to pay for discovering real treasure.

It is sometimes said that men and women look at the world in two different ways. Men look at the world in terms of objects. Women look at the same world in terms of relationships between objects. Perhaps a revolution is beginning to take place where men are starting to appreciate that it is relationships that might be more important. We must help men in particular drop the macho, self-sufficient image, and become soft enough to put people first. No matter how many digits in their salary I consider someone poor if they can never get to see their children perform in the school nativity play. There is another way to live, where true riches are to be found. We must call people, especially men, to drop false gods, including materialism. Jesus stated it boldly: 'You cannot serve both God and Money.'[5]

D. LUKE 19: 1–9: THE STORY OF ZACCHAEUS

If people have trouble finding any Good News in the incident of the rich man, the mistake they most commonly make when looking at the story of Zacchaeus is to read into the text what they have been taught. We need to be very careful when reading the Bible that we read out of it what it says, rather than put into it our theology. Whenever I do the exercise with a group I ask the question, 'What Good News did Jesus give to Zacchaeus?' Nearly always people skip over the Good News and jump straight to the end of the story. They quote the Good News as 'salvation has come to this house', adding that the Good News is about salvation from Zacchaeus' sinful life style. This demonstrates how some people's thinking is dominated by sin and salvation. True, salvation is announced at the end, but Jesus never mentions sin in the story. So what was the Good News that Jesus brought to Zacchaeus that resulted in his salvation? We need to look back far earlier in the story to find the Good News that Jesus brought to Zacchaeus, Good News that in turn brought Zacchaeus' response.

The Good News is contained in the first thing that Jesus says to Zacchaeus. With Zacchaeus perched up in the tree Jesus looks up and says: 'Zacchaeus, come down. Hurry, because I am to stay at your house today.' It is that sentence that contains the Good News which triggered such an enormous response in Zacchaeus. It is crucial to see that Jesus does not broach the subject of sin with Zacchaeus. He does not say: 'Zacchaeus, you are a sinner and a cheat, repent and follow me.' Jesus does say such things elsewhere, but not to Zacchaeus. Instead He simply says: 'I want to spend time with you.' That sentence must have been such shocking Good News to Zacchaeus I am surprised that he didn't fall out of the tree. Zacchaeus was a universally hated figure. Not only was he a tax collector, working for the occupying power, on a par with a Frenchman being a collaborator with the Nazis, but he was small! Imagine someone small, fat, balding, with B.O., bad breath and dandruff and you get the loathsome sort of figure that Zacchaeus represents. Rather like a traffic warden – nobody's friend. And Jesus, the most popular person in town, says He wants to come and stay at this person's house. Zacchaeus must have been desperately lonely, without a friend in the world. Rich, today he'd have a snooker-table, but no one to play with; a gold tea service, but nobody ever comes to tea. Until Jesus. The Good News for Zacchaeus is that Jesus is his friend. And from that simple statement of friendship and acceptance – a statement that Zacchaeus is valuable – flows all the rest. It is that Good News that brings about the transformation. Zacchaeus realizes in the face of such a friend just how evil and mean he is and he resolves to be different. Jesus doesn't have to mention sin, because in the light of friendship Zacchaeus cannot but change. Jesus' final statement emphasizes once again that Zacchaeus is acceptable and is included. Despised by his own people for working with the Romans, Jesus affirms that Zacchaeus still belongs to Israel: 'This man too is a son of Abraham.' Jesus, by simply befriending him, had brought back into the fold that which was lost.

Perhaps the most 'successful' evangelism takes place amongst first-year students as they start their university career. Apart from the fact that students are open-minded, exploring the world to discover new things, and therefore very open to all sorts of 'gospels', there is another reason why they are so open to Christianity. Loneliness. Most young people leaving home, often for the first time, and arriving in an unknown place amidst hordes of strangers, are very lonely. To these people the Good News is 'Jesus will be your friend, and the Church your home, where you can be with family, your brothers and sisters in Christ'. Churches in university towns will aim their message to address this theme of loneliness in order to appeal to the newcomer. And there is nothing wrong in doing so. It is a good example of applying the Gospel. Just as Jesus found the lonely Zacchaeus and offered to be his friend, we need to seek out the lost and the lonely and offer to befriend them, and include them in the family of the Church.

Ultimately this was the thread of Good News that my mother needed to hear and which I failed to tell her for two years and which God finally communicated in a dream. To preach this message of Jesus the friend as an answer to the issue of loneliness, is to preach only part of the Good News. It is perfectly valid but only in the appropriate circumstances. It would be folly, for instance, in an Asian culture with its enormously strong family networks, to concentrate on Jesus being a friend to the lonely. It would simply fall on deaf ears and it would be to present an irrelevant Gospel. We need a different Gospel for a different culture, a different Gospel for each individual. Alister McGrath summarizes it in his book *Justification by Faith*:

> The theme of 'Justification by Faith' is the fulfilment of human existence through the removal of the barriers that get placed in its path. To the individual who is preoccupied with guilt and knows that he cannot draw near to a Holy and righteous God, the word of forgiveness is spoken; through your faith in the death of Jesus Christ and His resurrection from the dead your sins are forgiven – rise, a forgiven sinner, and go forward into life and fellowship with your God! To the individual who is overwhelmed by a fear of death, the Gospel speaks the word of life; he who raised Christ Jesus from the dead will do the same for you – rejoice in that victory over death which is ours through Jesus Christ!. In short, there is a need to particularize the theme of justification in terms of the specific situation of those to whom it is proclaimed. The Gospel 'sameness' is not being eroded by doing so – we are merely drawing on the fullness of its remarkable resources.[6]

We must look at the broad package of Good News and assess which particular thread or theme will be most appropriate to those we wish to address. This brings me back to a crucial point that I have mentioned earlier, but which I wish to emphasize. It means we must get to know somebody in order to select the appropriate thread of Good News. You cannot be relevant until you understand the particular situation in which an individual finds himself. Hence we must befriend and listen *before* offering Good News. It is frequently said that we must earn the right to speak. We are given two ears and only one mouth, so perhaps we need to listen twice as long before speaking.

Perhaps the story of Zacchaeus carries an especially important point about how we should evangelize in the twentieth century. Jesus' approach to Zacchaeus reminds us that we must befriend the sinful, evil people, and must go out and spend time with them, getting to know them, valuing them, accepting and including them, and trusting that our love will bring about the change that we long to see in them. We must not increase their alienation but must with love draw them back into the fold. Yet all too frequently the Church is perceived to be judgmental and exclusive. A club for the self-righteous and pious, filled with people who act as if they believe they are good enough while the rest are pagan sinners. We must work hard to change this perception. How dare we refuse to accept people before they have repented and before they agree to our doctrines. The model of Christ is to mingle with and invite Himself to stay with sinners, while they are still sinners. We must not forget that 'While we were still sinners, Christ died for us'.[7] We have got our evangelism the wrong way round. We act as if we will have nothing to do with people until after they have repented, whereas Jesus does exactly the opposite. He has everything to do with sinners before they repent. Indeed it is His association with them, His acceptance and love of them, that initiates their repentance and salvation. That is the example of Jesus. Let us imitate it.

HIS-STORY, OUR STORY

In the Sunday colour magazines there are nearly always several offers for different gadgets designed to help you get fit. When I was young the exercise gadget then in vogue for men was a chest expander. A number of tightly coiled springs with handles at each end was designed so that you were supposed to expand it to its full potential when holding it in front of you. It amused me that these chest expanders were guaranteed. They guaranteed that after a few months pulling you would be able to expand the springs much further. What they didn't tell you of course was that this would be due, not so much to you getting stronger, but to the springs getting weaker! Guaranteed progress.

The solution to a small and weak chest is exercise. The solution to a shrunken Gospel which is such a weakness in evangelism is exercise. We need to do some exercises to help us to expand our awareness of the Good News. I remember a conversation with my vicar that took place shortly after putting myself forward for the ordained ministry. We were talking about the different things a vicar had to do, and the importance of preaching. 'The thing that worries me', I said, 'is how do you have enough to say every Sunday. I'll have run out of things to preach about by the end of my first month.' He smiled. 'I don't think it will be a problem. When you've been on the Christian

journey a bit longer you'll find there are plenty of things to say.'
Looking above my desk at the nine ring-binder files containing
my sermons, I know he is right but I was genuinely afraid that I
would run out of material for preaching.

There are numerous reasons why people are tongue-tied
when it comes to talking about their Christian faith. One is
that they are not confident that they have enough to talk about.
At the Sunday services on our missions I usually get someone
to stand at the front and say something about why they are a
Christian. When I ask people if they are willing to be interviewed in this way the most common reply is 'But I'll dry up, I
just won't know what to say.' I always say to these people, 'Fine,
if you haven't got a lot to say, say a little. Brevity is beautiful.
You will probably be a good antidote to the vicar.' (I can say
that because I am one!) When I finish interviewing them, the
majority respond by saying, 'But I'd hardly got started.' People
have far more to say than they realize, and talking about ourselves is not nearly as difficult as we think, especially when
prompted by an interviewer.

We have got plenty of material to share because the Good
News concerns God's action. And God has acted often and
very clearly. We have more than enough to talk about. The
same dread of not having enough material occurred at school
when I was doing exams. I would think ahead to the three-hour
examination paper and say to myself, 'I'll never have enough to
say to keep me going that long.' What utter nonsense. Only
three hours to sum up what I had been taught for eight hours a
week for the past two years! I had masses of material – what I
needed was some revision of that material to remind me just
how much I had to put down. We could do with some revision
classes, or recollection exercises, to prepare ourselves for evan-

gelism. Most important of all we need history revision ...
His-story revision.

We have a story to tell, or rather we have two stories to
tell. We have first and foremost to tell the story of God and of
what God has done in the past: His-story. It is a story
of creation and sustenance, of God's involvement and care for
His world. It is a story of how God acts; the creation of a race
out of an enslaved people, the giving to them of a promised
land, and also the weighty responsibility to share their understanding of God with all people. It is a story of the ups and
downs of people struggling to be faithful to a God who is
always faithful; the story of men and women who pleaded and
argued and bullied and persuaded (and failed to persuade)
their people to return to a relationship with God (these were
the prophets). And centrally it is the story of what God did in
order to woo us back, to win back the love of a faithless people.
The story of how God spoke through the prophets, telling of
His love for His people, but then decided to act. The story of a
God who knew that actions speak louder than words. We must
tell of the God who left the heavens and who came down to
earth to be born to a poor, simple girl in a backwater in Judea;
who humbled Himself and became a man; the creator becoming part of creation in order to communicate face to face; the
story of Jesus, His life and words; His abandonment and death,
and His rising from the dead and ascension back into Heaven.
It is a story which comes to a climax in the four gospels and the
first chapter of Acts.

There is no short cut to His-story revision. We must go back
to the primary sources, the texts themselves. We must read
the Bible. We must pore over it until it sinks deep into our
consciousness. And it is not just a question of reading the
Bible, we need to study it. We need to read it with our full

attention, probing it, bringing our questions and difficulties to it, demanding something from our reading rather than simply letting the words wash over us. There are numerous study guides and commentaries available which will assist us in our Bible reading however little time we have available, and whatever our level of intellect. And we must read the whole of the Bible. Some so-called 'mature' Christians have a rather dismissive attitude to the gospels. They consider them rather a light diet compared to the 'richer meat' of the Pauline epistles such as Romans. This is arrogant nonsense. It is no accident that in the liturgical churches, whatever other readings we may have at the Eucharist, the readings always reach their climax in the reading of the Gospel. Also we must not shy away from reading the Old Testament. The Old and New Testaments are a united whole, and we need to work at integrating the Old Testament into the Christian story. We should not see them as two distinct eras, but as one story which reaches its culmination in Christ. In a nutshell, the Old Testament describes how mankind was created with a beautiful relationship with God. We turned away from God bringing destruction and death to everything in our world. But God did not abandon us. God had a rescue plan to restore the relationship. The Old Testament talks of a 'Rescuer' who will one day come and rescue us from the consequences of our own stupidity. The New Testament begins with the birth of Jesus the Rescuer and carries on to reveal God's audacious and risky plan. Thus the two halves of the Bible are inextricably linked. And we must study both. Chest expanders only work if used regularly. If we were to read our Bibles daily and to be asking constantly what Good News is contained in it, then our understanding of the Gospel would expand enormously – I guarantee it!

Anybody who has tried revising for exams will know that one

enemy of study is boredom, and this can be a big problem with reading the Bible. Perhaps this is not surprising; familiarity breeds not necessarily contempt but certainly complacency. I've known people who have brought their Bible to a talk, but when the speaker announces which passage they say, 'Oh I know that bit', and don't bother to open their Bible. It is difficult not to switch off mentally when parables which we have known from school days are read as the lessons in our churches. We need to revitalise our enthusiasm for Bible reading and to allow the pages of the Bible to come back to life. It may help to get a new Bible – literally. Buy a new Bible and make sure you get a different version. The different words used in different translations will jump out at us and open our eyes to new meanings, giving us fresh insights. Certainly my Bible reading was greatly enhanced after five years as a Christian when I purchased a *New Jerusalem Bible*. This was not only because of the freshness of its translation and the difference of its layout, but doubly so because it contained extensive footnotes.

Whatever tools and techniques we decide to use, it is of paramount importance that we become familiar with the story of God's activity told in the pages of the Bible.

Recollection is a lost art. We live in an age of immediacy in which storytelling is dying out and in which history, including our own personal history, is being forgotten or ignored. This is in marked contrast to what you would find in Bible times. One of the Canticles that is used every day at Evensong in the Anglican Church is the Magnificat: The song of Mary. The frequency of its use is appropriate not only because it draws us back to the incarnation as we recall Gabriel's announcement to Mary that she would give birth to God Incarnate. But also because the Magnificat gives a reminder, a pocket summary, of the actions of God in the past:

> He has stretched out his mighty arm and scattered the proud with all their plans. He has brought down mighty kings from their thrones, and lifted up the lowly. He has filled the hungry with good things, and sent the rich away with empty hands. He has kept the promise he made to our ancestors, and has come to the help of his servant Israel. He has remembered to show mercy to Abraham and to all his descendants for ever![1]

Mary, as a Jewess of her time, was steeped in scripture – the story of God acting – History. And the history of the Jewish people is the story of God at work in His world intervening on behalf of the poor and the needy to bring liberation, freedom and life to people. The Jewish people were a people very conscious of their identity because they were conscious of their history. Jews were good at recollecting and at reciting. At every Passover the history would be recited afresh and celebrated. The Mishnah sets out what is to happen;

> the son asks his father (and if the son has not enough understanding, his father instructs him how to ask), 'Why is this night different from other nights? For on other nights we eat seasoned food once, but this night twice; on other nights we eat leavened or unleavened bread, but this night all is unleavened; on other nights we eat fresh roast stewed, or cooked, but this night all is roast.' And according to the understanding of the son, his father instructs him. He begins with the disgrace and ends with the glory; and he expounds from 'a wandering Aramaean was my father . . .'

(Deuteronomy 26: 5–11) until he finishes the whole section.'[2]

It is this history which gives the Jewish people their identity. But it is not simply a case of reciting an ancient history to remind themselves of their past. The Jewish people have a very profound relationship with their history because they regard themselves as being involved IN it. At the end of the recitation the Mishnah concludes:

In every generation a man must so regard himself as if he came forth himself out of Egypt, for it is written, 'And thou shalt tell thy son in that day saying, It is because of that which the Lord did for me when I came forth out of Egypt'. Therefore we are bound to give thanks, to praise, to glorify, to honour, to exalt, to extol, and to bless him who wrought all these wonders for our fathers and for us.[3]

Our praise and enthusiasm for God should grow naturally from an awareness of what He has done for us. At all times, but especially when we are going through difficult or low patches, we need to be aware of what God has done in the past and this will give us the strength and confidence to press ahead. Our faith needs to be rooted in these two stories, or histories. Firstly, in the history of salvation, what God did in forming His people in the Old Testament which reached its fulfilment and climax in the story of Jesus. And secondly in our own history – the story of how God met, embraced, challenged, comforted and called us personally.

For there is another story to tell: The story of what has happened since the Bible was written, and most important what has happened to me. The second story in a way is a commentary on the first. A comment on the issue of 'so what?' To anyone who might question the relevance of the Christian story because it all happened so long ago, the answer is found in the second sort of story. For the second story tells what difference the first story makes to the likes of you and me today. We need to reflect in depth on our own story. To recollect the story of our own faith and to use this in talking to others. We need to broaden our awareness of the many and varied ways that God has acted in our lives.

Before each of the missions I ask the members of my team to write out a spiritual and secular curriculum vitae. Part of my aim is purely practical – during a mission week I will want to use different people to tell a snippet of their lifestory, drawing out different points in the form of a testimony. Having a written account from each member of the team means that I only need to flick through the pages to find which person it would be best to pick upon. But as well as this immediate practical benefit there is another excellent reason for asking people to write down their stories just prior to a mission. Most of the people whom I ask have never actually written out a brief history of their spiritual journey before. At first they are daunted by the idea and think it will be a hard slog to produce something. But as they do it they discover the encouragement of looking back and seeing what God has done for them in the past. Not only are they then more ready to talk about it, having brought specific memories to mind, but they are also more expectant about seeing God act in the future. John Finney's research backs this up:

> More than 500 people took part. For most it was the first time that they had had an opportunity to talk in an ordered

way about their faith. *They found it helpful to trace the hand of God in their lives* (emphasis mine).[4]

Each of us should carry out a simple exercise in recollection. This can be done by writing down a straightforward chronological account, either looking backwards or starting at any point we like and writing down the key points at which we have been conscious of God working in our lives. The process might be helped by doing it on a chart like this:

GOOD		
	BIRTH	**TODAY**
BAD		

I encourage people to look back to each period of their lives and put in both the good and the bad things that happened. To include the 'spiritual' and the 'nonspiritual'. Then to add where they were particularly aware of God, and where they felt His presence.

When I first did this I found it quite difficult. We were set this sort of exercise during a community retreat here at Lee Abbey. The warden gave a talk on recollection, then sent us off for the next hour to do it – to sit down and recollect just what God has done for me. I sat down for twenty minutes staring at the blank piece of paper thinking, 'I am grateful for my wife and I enjoy my job, which I know God led me to, and there it stops.' But suddenly after twenty minutes it was as if the dam on my imagination cracked and then burst. For the next forty minutes I wrote almost non-stop, one thing flowing on from another, filling a whole sheet of paper with different reminiscences of what God had done in my life. I was truly able to praise and thank God and also felt so much more confident facing the future (which was the next part of the retreat; after looking back we looked forward). Unless we pause in the rush through life and recollect, we can remain very unaware of just how much we have to be grateful for. Worship, particularly worship that is based on a liturgical cycle and which goes through the different seasons of the Christian year, should be a very powerful reminder of all that God has done for us and also of what He has promised to accomplish in the future. In the same way that the Passover reminded the Jews what God did for them in rescuing them from Egypt, our worship and particularly the Holy Communion remind us of what God has done for us. Our worship should week by week act as a revision class, reminding us of the story of God's saving action and providing us with endless material for evangelism!

One continuous way of recollecting and thus expanding our awareness of the Good News, and what we have to be grateful for, is to keep a journal. The work of Ira Progoff, perhaps the best-known present-day champion of journalling, provides many exercises to help in the creation of a journal. Of course, it need not be a written account at all. We do not all think or express ourselves best in language. Drawing or scribbling, whether of any artistic merit or not, can be very helpful as a means of exploring and expressing our journey. After our missions, when we work with the churches to review and assess how it went, we always ask members to draw what was most memorable for them about the mission week. After the usual protests of 'I can't draw', people come up with the most extraordinary scribbles which for them (and this is the whole point) captures something that cannot adequately be expressed in words.

Another marvellous way to increase our appreciation of story, and history, is to use individuals in telling their stories in our church services. In some traditions the 'sharing of testimonies' is well known, whereas in other churches no one does anything upfront, even read the lesson, let alone talk of their experience of God. We are missing out on a vital and valuable jewel in our church life, when we fail to tell the stories about what God has done and is doing today. Even the churches that do have a tradition of getting individuals up to the front to tell their 'story' tend to allow only a very limited type of testimony. We need to be imaginative, to go beyond simply telling how I got converted, and to also tell about what has happened since. And we must dare to include the down sides as well as the up sides. After all, if Jesus said 'the way to heaven is narrow and difficult'[5], then we need to own up to that when we give our accounts of the Christian pilgrimage. And we need to find creative ways to do it. We should learn from television that it is far better to interview people than simply to allow them to stand up in front and rabbit on. Most monologues are monotonous, whereas dialogue is delightful. The 'Songs of Praise' formula, which gets someone to choose a hymn or a song, and then explain why they have chosen it, is brilliantly effective. It works because it is based on the obvious truth that people are nosey and most interested in finding out about other people. In writing a book such as this, I have been constantly encouraged not to talk in concepts but to use anecdotes. It is the human stories that really get the point across.

The Diocese of Manchester devised a training course to help people get back in touch with and tell their own story. One session was built around the old and very popular television programme 'This is Your Life'. Perhaps an occasional series in our churches introducing us to different members of the congregation and doing a 'This is Your Life' would provide a way of rediscovering and retelling our histories. Ask yourself what you know at all about even the leading members of your congregation like the churchwardens or elders. Do you know what they do for a living, let alone anything about the route which God has taken them in their journey of faith? Jesus told us not to keep our light hidden under a bushel, but to let people see it. We need to pluck up courage and tell each other, as well as outsiders, the difference that God has made in our lives. We need the courage to share ourselves.

One of the greatest privileges and most exciting things that happens when I take teams out to work with churches is that members of the church we are visiting begin to tell their story and even dare to tell it to one another. Recently, on a trip to Arundel in West Sussex, I stayed with the churchwarden. On the Sunday morning, quite unprompted by any of us, the six-year-old daughter of one of the members of the team asked him 'Just what is a Christian then?' The churchwarden told me later that this was the first time in his life he had ever had to speak directly on the subject, but he was proud because he believed he had managed to answer the question. I was proud that, almost accidentally, we had given him the opportunity; proud that he was able to respond to it; and thrilled that for him, too, the dam had burst and he had begun to talk about his faith.

6

SHARING OURSELVES

Sharing our story will involve far more than simply telling people facts. It means sharing ourselves. When God wanted to communicate He became a human being. To get through to people God knew that the ultimate form of communication was face to face. He did not send a letter or a telegram, because neither method is good enough. The only way to communicate about love is in person. The message He brought is all about relationship and the method He employed then was to come and relate. God has not changed His technique of communication. God sends not letters but people to show and tell of His love. He sends you and me.

Most people do not meet Jesus in a place. No, usually they see Jesus in a person, an ordinary person like you or me. It is one of the hardest things of all to believe, that you and I are capable of revealing Jesus to people. But it is true. It may be rather like one of those 'Halls of Mirrors' that you find at the end of a seaside pier. You stand in front of the mirror and get a good laugh as you shrink to a midget or expand with legs like a giraffe. The image is a bit distorted but it is still recognizably you. We reflect a distorted picture of Jesus, but it is nevertheless recognizable. We know some people show the reality of Jesus in their lives. We can all think of 'saints', great people like Mother Teresa who personify Christ. And we can also think of ordinary people, people we have known ourselves, who have shown Jesus to us. I remember watching a Christian singer give a concert and thinking, 'If Jesus is anything like that, I can't wait to meet Him.' The man simply glowed, and transmitted the beauty of God. We know other people can show Jesus in their lives, but it is far harder for us to believe that Jesus can be seen in me. The fact is that the best picture some people will get of Jesus is you and me. But do not despair, because Jesus is perfectly capable of revealing Himself through even the likes of you and me.

The startling truth is that if you are a Christian, and if you talk to other people, then you are automatically being evangelistic. This may sound odd, but I believe Scripture backs it up. I base this idea on a passage in Paul's second letter to the Corinthians. It is a passage in which Paul gives his definition of a Christian – in which he lays down the bench marks for faith. Paul says it's not whether you go to church, not whether you read the Bible, not even whether you are good that counts. It's not external things that determine whether you are a Christian, rather it's a question of whether or not Jesus dwells in you:

Examine yourselves to see whether you are in the faith; test yourselves. Do you not realize that Christ Jesus is in you – unless, of course, you fail the test?'[1]

A Christian according to Paul is someone in whom Christ lives. This theme is beautifully portrayed in Holman Hunt's painting *The Light of the World* based on Revelation 3:20 which is perhaps the most used evangelistic verse of all time:

Here I am! I stand at the door and knock. If anyone hears

my voice and opens the door, I will come in and eat with
him, and he with me.

That is the definition of a Christian; someone who has opened
the door of their life to Jesus Christ, someone in whom Jesus
lives.

This definition of a Christian as someone in whom Jesus is
dwelling has enormous ramifications for evangelism. For if
Jesus dwells in you, then when you share yourself, you will be
sharing Jesus automatically. When people meet me for the first
time it doesn't take them very long to find out that I am a keen
golfer, and that I have a son, Edward, a daughter called
Harriet, and a lovely wife called Lucy. Golf is part of my life,
and Edward, Harriet and Lucy are very much part of my
life, and I cannot prevent myself from bringing them into the
conversation when talking with other people. Of course I may
not mention them straight away, but sooner or later people are
bound to find out about them.

The same is true for Jesus. Jesus is the centre of my life and
though it may not be the first thing people find out, inevitably
once they get to know me they will discover this too. All you
have to do to share Jesus is to share yourself. This is what Paul
claimed he had done in Thessalonica:

We loved you so much that we were delighted to share with
you not only the Gospel of God but our lives as well . . .[2]

Evangelism means sharing yourself. This is certainly the model
we are shown by Jesus. Jesus came down from Heaven and
dwelt among us. He humbled Himself, as the second chapter
of Philippians reminds us; God coming to live cheek by jowl
with ordinary human beings. For three years He lived in a sort

67

of wandering community with His disciples and the women who also followed Him. With these people and with the others He met on His journeys He shared Himself. He allowed people to get close and see Him as he really was. The portrait we are given in the gospels is of a totally open and vulnerable person. Jesus is fully human; while journeying through Samaria He gets thirsty and tired; He weeps at the tomb of Lazarus, and over Jerusalem. And He allows His disciples and others to minister to Him in His weakness, even allowing His feet to be washed. Jesus is fully open, being quite prepared to allow people to see Him as He really is. Are we prepared to follow Jesus' example and allow people to get close to us?

We are to be sent out to others in exactly the same way that Jesus was sent to us. The command to evangelize as recorded in John is short and to the point:

As the Father has sent me, I am sending you: [3]

Jesus and the Incarnation are to be the model for our evangelism. For us to imitate Jesus means we are to go with that sort of humility, vulnerability and openness. Will we dare to take His lead and let people see us as we really are, in our frail human vulnerability?

It is very difficult to be known for who we are. Being real is painful and costly. Perhaps this is why so little real evangelism takes place. For here lies the real cost of evangelism. To be prepared to share yourself is to take a risk. But it is the only way to evangelize. This is the high price that is demanded of us.

We are afraid of our humanity. And there lies the real difficulty in evangelism because sharing ourselves is very far from being easy. I live and work on the Lee Abbey Community in

North Devon, one of the largest religious communities in this country, numbering some seventy people. When we become full members of the community (after a period of probation) we take seven promises. All of our community agree which is the most difficult of these vows. It is the one where we promise to be real with one another. As we stand at the front of the chapel with the rest of the community standing around us we are asked

> Are you prepared to learn to live in fellowship, being open to be known for what we are, accepting one another in Christ, and saying of others nothing that could not be said to them personally if love and wisdom required it?

Being real is extremely hard. It is not insignificant that on becoming full members of community we change the badge we wear from green to red. Our warden frequently points out that newcomers wear green, the colour of naivety, because they usually expect living on a Christian community to be bliss. After three months we switch to red, to remind us how bloody it is – making Christians live together is a business that inevitably results in the shedding of blood.

It is difficult to befriend people because it is difficult to become vulnerable enough to allow them to get close to us. Being a friend means allowing people to get close enough to see the real you, allowing them to get behind the layers of masks that are normally kept firmly in place to protect people from seeing us as we really are.

The conversations we hold are all too often used as means of keeping people at arm's length. We are careful to keep most conversations at a very superficial level, only allowing those closest to us to get below the surface. On the Community we have a joke about the superficiality of the conversations that take place on the first night of any house party. The two questions we are asked by our guests are; 'How long have you been on Community?' and 'What will you do when you leave?' We hate this because we know it doesn't help us to get to know them, but we are just as guilty of keeping the conversation at a banal level. The two questions we ask them are: 'Did you have a good trip down?' and 'Have you been to Lee Abbey before?' There is of course nothing wrong in starting at a banal level of conversation, as long as we move on to something more substantial. The reason we dislike it is because all too often the discussion goes nowhere.

Conversation can be likened to different layers. On the surface we have what amounts to nothing more than a greeting: 'Hi, how are you?' but we do not expect a real answer, and everyone knows this, which is why we always reply 'fine' even if we're feeling lousy. One layer below the surface we have an exchange of information. This is very safe because it involves merely the swapping of cold facts: 'The vicar has announced that he is leaving.' We go one layer deeper in conversation when we exchange not just cold information but when we share how someone else feels about the situation: 'Mrs Smith the churchwarden is chuffed that the vicar has resigned at last.' Quite obviously conversing at this level is far more risky and opens us up to the possibility of being misunderstood. However we are still only talking about what other people think. The next layer of conversation takes place when we talk about what we ourselves think or feel about something; 'I'm really sad the vicar has decided to leave and I'll miss him enormously.' This is opening ourselves out and making ourselves quite vulnerable. The deepest and most intimate layer of conversation takes place when we share what we are feeling, not about something, but what we are feeling about ourselves: 'I feel really lost and empty inside.'

We need to be aware of how we manipulate language to keep people at arm's length. Becoming aware of the different layers of our conversation can help us to become more vulnerable and more real when we are talking to people. This does not mean that we should always talk at the most intimate level – always sharing how we feel about ourselves. That would be rather similar to constantly uprooting a pot plant to see how it is growing. But we need to be aware of the times when we are refusing to allow people to get close to us, and be challenged by Jesus' example to allow some degree of vulnerability. Furthermore if we find that all our relationships are lived at the shallowest level, and there is no one with whom we share at a deeper level, then we should seek help, lest we shrivel and die from lack of real human contact.

I believe that most of us are afraid to be ourselves; our real selves that is. We are like onions; made up of several layers. If you peel away the layers of an onion you will find at the core a soft juicy centre. People are the same. Below the layers is a soft and beautiful person. The reason I put on layers is fear. I am afraid that people will not accept or like the real me. I am afraid of their rejection which will hurt a great deal. So I put on a protective layer which has two functions. Firstly, the protective layer is intended to stop people getting too close, to prevent them finding out what the real me is like so they can't reject me. Secondly, the layer is intended to present to the world a nice me, something that I think people will like. The layer presents a façade, a false me in order to attract positive comments. Now there are a couple of problems with this strategy. Firstly, I find keeping up this façade very difficult, because I am caught in the tension of wanting to show the real me. I want to be valued for who I really am. Also I feel deceitful. I know it is not the real me, and being accepted for a false front is not really very rewarding. So I am caught in a tension. I want to remove the protective layer, but I'm not sure that I dare risk doing so.

Being real is a risky business. When should I let people see the real me? It is rather like gambling (and here I had better explain for the benefit of those Christians who are not too familiar with how to gamble). In gambling you have a choice of two strategies; there is a high-risk strategy where there is a potential for high reward but there is also a high risk. Or there is a strategy where you can play relatively safe. You don't stand to win as much but then you have far less risk of losing. If you have for example £10 to bet on a horse then you can place all of the £10 on the horse to win. If your horse should win then you will do very well and make a fat profit, but if your horse comes second even by just a whisker then you lose everything. The alternative method is called 'each-way betting'. Taking the same £10 you put £5 on the horse to win and £5 on the horse should it be placed in the first three or four runners. If your horse should come first you will not win as much as you could have done had you bet all £10 on it to win. However, if your horse comes second or third then you still stand to make some profit. In approaching life and love we can adopt either of these two strategies. We can go out and risk everything. If we are accepted then we experience great joy, but if we are rejected then the price is extreme pain. Alternatively, we can play safe. We don't run the risk of experiencing such pain but equally we will never discover the heights of joy.

The negative experiences of life push us in the direction of playing safe. When someone rejects us we put up another façade, adding another layer to the onion. And so the chain reaction begins, and the protective layers build up around my real self. I end up being covered with layers protecting other layers . . . until the real me is buried way down below the surface, well out of harm's way. I am well protected from being seen and most importantly prevented from getting hurt. But I get so buried under the layers that the real me cannot breathe, it suffocates and dies. Swamped by the masks we wear, we can lose sight of the real person beneath them.

Now when you describe it like that it may seem a silly strategy. But the problem is that we live in a fallen world, and the fear that starts the chain off, the fear of being hurt, is a very reasonable one. We do get hurt, people are horrible to us and they do reject us. The problem is that when we build walls to protect ourselves we end up not being able to get out. We end up being shut off completely. The walls that you use to protect you from getting hurt also bar you from receiving love, and without love, you die. How do we stop this chain reaction? We don't – Jesus does.

Jesus came to bring us back to life. To help us to live, to live fully: 'I have come that they may have life, and have it to the full'.[4] He came to liberate us from the chains that are self-imposed, to set us free to love once again. He came to knock down the walls that bar us from one another:

For he himself is our peace, who has made the two one and has destroyed the barrier, the dividing wall of hostility, by abolishing in his flesh the law with its commandments and regulations. His purpose was to create in Himself one new person out of the two, thus making peace, and in this one body to reconcile both of them to God through the cross, by which he put to death their hostility.[5]

Jesus came to redeem mankind, to restore us, to free us to be ourselves, to be authentic. The means whereby He did so is by loving us overpoweringly, loving us just as we really are. He cuts through the onion layers and bursts His love upon the real self buried down deep beneath, saying, 'I love you and accept you – the real you'.

On the Cross, Jesus showed what He felt for the real person. However grotty you feel about yourself He says, 'I love you this much. I love you enough to die for you. I will pay this price to liberate the real you so that I can have you to love.' But the Cross is not a comfortable or easy place to go to. For the Cross is double-edged. It is the place where you will find out just how much you are loved and accepted, but it is also the place where you will discover your ugliness. I found this out in a staff meeting when I was a curate. We were praying at the end of our meeting just before lunch. During a moment of silence a horrible picture flashed into my mind. It was of Jesus' back after it had been whipped being lowered against the wooden beam of the Cross. It was a disgusting sight. The only way I can describe it is to say that it was bright purple, resembling a piece of meat after it has been pummelled with a steak hammer. As His back touched the wood I flinched and said (inside my head): 'I don't want that to be my fault.' Quick as a flash a voice came back, (again inside my head): 'But it is.' I carried on watching the scene in my mind, very upset and on the verge of tears, when the voice went on: 'But I love you this much.' Then I knew how much I was loved. Jesus loved the grottiest bits of me enough to go to these extremes to show it. When I faced the ugliest bits of me and then heard that He loves me, then I became secure in His love. This is the meaning behind Paul's statement:

God demonstrates His own love for us in this: while we were still sinners, Christ died for us.[6]

It is only when we have encountered that love, been accepted by the unconditional love of Jesus, that we will be able to break through the barriers that separate us from other people. It is finding that security, that love, that acceptance by Jesus of the real you that enables you to run the high risk, enables you to be real, enables you to live. It is because we know in the light of Jesus' death on the Cross that God loves us just as we are, that we can face the world as we are. We can have a new confidence that we really are lovable.

But the onion layers, the façades that we have built up over the years, do not necessarily drop away instantly. Like the grave clothes of Lazarus after Jesus had resurrected him, they need to be taken off, and this frequently requires the help of other people and taking them off will be painful. If you peel onions, what happens? You cry. In the process of becoming real, tears will almost always be shed and you will be made more vulnerable. But that very process of allowing vulnerability to flood in will itself be evangelistic. People will notice and wonder where you find the strength to be authentic. You can tell them the answer lies in the love of Jesus Christ shown on the Cross. What you need to be effective in evangelism is nothing more or less than this: to be you. For in you people will see the Living God.

This is beautifully expressed in a powerful parable written in the 1920's by Margery Williams called *The Velveteen Rabbit*.

'What is REAL?' asked the Rabbit one day, when they were lying side by side near the nursery fender, before Nana came to tidy the room. 'Does it mean having things that buzz inside you and a stick-out handle?'

'Real isn't how you are made,' said the Skin Horse. 'It's a thing that happens to you. When a child loves you for a long,

long time, not just to play with, but REALLY loves you, then you become Real.'

'Does it hurt?' asked the Rabbit.

'Sometimes,' said the Skin Horse, for he was always truthful. 'When you are Real you don't mind being hurt.'

'Does it happen all at once, like being wound up,' he asked, 'or bit by bit?'

'It doesn't happen all at once,' said the Skin Horse. 'You become. It takes a long time. That's why it doesn't often happen to people who break easily, or have sharp edges, or who have to be carefully kept. Generally by the time you are Real, most of your hair has been loved off, and your eyes drop out and you get loose in the joints and very shabby. But these things don't matter, except to people who don't understand.'

'I suppose you are Real?' asked the Rabbit. And then he wished he had not said it, for he thought the Skin Horse might be sensitive. But the Skin Horse only smiled.

'The Boy's Uncle made me Real,' he said. 'That was a great many years ago; but once you are Real you can't become unreal again. It lasts for ever.'[7]

The challenge if you want to evangelize is the challenge to dare to be real. In *The Horse and His Boy*, another children's story by C. S. Lewis, the horse Bree finally comes to meet Aslan the Lion, and is too terrified to turn round. The words Aslan uses to encourage him I also use to encourage you to make the journey into reality. Aslan said: 'Do not dare not to dare.'

7

PRAYER

The very first thing we should do about evangelism is to pray. We should pray for the courage to share our faith and to share ourselves. We should pray for opportunities to make friends and to share with those friends every part of ourselves including the spiritual dimension. We should pray for guidance about when to speak and when to remain silent; guidance as to which thread of Good News to pass on to a particular person. Prayer should always precede evangelism. But as well as using prayer as a preparation for sharing our faith, perhaps we should also use it as a means of doing so. Here I believe lies one of the richest seams of evangelistic potential, a veritable goldmine of opportunity, and yet it is a seam that is virtually untouched. For most of our evangelistic energy has gone into bombarding people with facts rather than helping them learn how to pray. John Finney wrote in his report:

> Prayer is such a common experience, even among those who have no practice of churchgoing, that the ways in which we can evangelize by helping people with their prayer life need to be explored.[1]

It might seem natural to reserve prayer as a subject to be discussed with people *after* they have been converted. But I believe prayer gives us enormous opportunities for evangelizing those yet to become Christians. Far from being reserved for the believer, prayer can be the first topic of conversation with those hovering on the edges of faith.

Prayer is a good choice of topic in evangelism for several reasons. First, in my experience most people are fascinated by prayer. They want to know what happens when we do it. People are nosey when it comes to hearing about other people's prayers: 'Do you hear voices?' 'What do you mean God guides you?' 'Just exactly how do you feel God communicated with you?' 'Describe this peace you get when you pray.' 'How do you hear God speaking to you?'

If ever I want to guarantee having a lively debate with non-Christians then I talk about prayer. People seem perfectly happy to ask questions about our praying and are fascinated by our answers. Secondly, the subject of prayer offers a goldmine of opportunity for evangelism because most people have some experience of doing it. Most people pray. The figures about prayer are quite extraordinary; more people pray than actually own up to a belief in God. I have always wondered who they are praying to, or rather who they think they are praying to! Thirdly, prayer is the most natural subject for evangelism because it gets at the very heart of what evangelism is trying to achieve. The aim of all our evangelistic endeavour is that the person develops a personal relationship with Jesus Christ. Prayer is at the very heart of that personal relationship. Therefore to talk about prayer, and to help someone to pray, is automatically to be bringing them into a closer relationship and therefore automatically evangelistic.

Prayer is far from easy. From the earliest days of my conversion people have been at pains to stress to me the vital importance of the 'quiet-time'. In sermons and in personal conversations everybody I met would emphasize to me how essential it was to set aside a quiet half-hour, preferably at the start of the day, to spend in prayer with God. But though everyone I met stressed its importance, no one I talked to had anything very positive to offer that helped me to develop this quiet period of prayer. Before my conversion I had not, apart from the occasional desperate plea, prayed for thirty seconds in a month, let alone for thirty minutes each and every day. It seemed an eternity. What was I supposed to do? Or more interestingly, what did other people do? – For surely everyone was getting it right and was managing to achieve a deep prayer life (whatever that was) – whereas I would sit, stare at the wall, daydream, close my eyes, or even (sin of all sins) fall asleep. I seemed unable to concentrate on the task in hand, partly perhaps because I was not sure what the task in hand was. What was I supposed to be doing?

Occasionally these difficulties about praying were aired in our church discussion groups when people were brave and honest enough to admit that they too struggled. But nothing very constructive was offered apart from the injunction to be disciplined. The only recommendation I heard about *how* to pray (rather than just the need to pray) was the acronym ACTS: adore – confess – thank – supplicate. The correct order of activity for prayer was to start by adoring God – praising and worshipping Him for who He is. Then in response to God's beauty and holiness experienced in the act of adoration we would be moved naturally to confess our sinfulness. Supplication or requests should come last of all after a time of thanksgiving, a thanksgiving which would flow naturally from having confessed and received forgiveness. I tried it but it didn't work, for two reasons. First I didn't know how to adore or for that matter confess. My concepts of both, perhaps not surprisingly for a young Christian, were very limited, and when repeated daily became desperately repetitive, which meant that prayer following this formula quickly became dull ritual. And secondly it didn't work because applying the formula took no account of *me*, who I was, where I was at in my spiritual journey, or how I was feeling. (The last point about 'feeling' I was warned about, being told we shouldn't rely on our feelings.) With this the only suggested method I quite quickly stopped praying. I was still having the quiet half-hour, but I wasn't praying during it. Instead, frustrated, I would make a half-hearted attempt to go through the formula and then spend the rest of the time reading my Bible, good value in itself but not prayer. It was only when I owned up to this and the dissatisfaction that it was causing that I was able to do anything. I went and sought help, something which was not easy to find.

What I needed was real, rather than formulaic, guidance. Guidance from somebody who had learnt how to struggle in prayer and who knew how to make suggestions that I could experiment with and which I could try out. I needed a 'spiritual director', someone to guide me as I explored the path of prayer, someone who had journeyed ahead down the same route, who had himself been down some dead ends, most importantly someone who could encourage me at my pace.

If I need a guide to learn how to pray after becoming a Christian how much more do those who have yet to be converted need some guidance? People need help to pray and the help they need is personal. We need encouragement from friends to be able to press on with praying. Yes I have read books on prayer some of which have helped significantly to overcome the various hurdles I have met on my prayer pilgrimage, but nothing has helped me as much as being able to talk honestly and openly with other people about the problems I have encountered in my prayer life.

The reason we need help is because praying is difficult. It is hard to have the discipline to get down to it – it seems everything conspires against prayer being easy and on a spiritual level I am sure that a battle takes place every time someone thinks of praying, a battle waged to try and prevent the prayer ever getting started. And prayer becomes more problematic the more we do it. It is difficult day after day to sit and talk to God without becoming stale and unimaginative. Our prayer life constantly needs refreshing and overhauling and will do so until we die.

Prayer is also difficult because God makes it difficult. When I went on the selection conference run by the Church of England to determine whether I was suitable to become a vicar I was interviewed by five people, including the now Bishop of Oxford, Richard Harries, then Dean of King's, London – a person who was sufficiently awe-inspiring and intimidating, more especially to someone like myself who had by then only been attending church for just over a year and a half. His first question of the interview was short and direct – 'How is your prayer life?' I had decided before even setting out for the interviews that I would be one hundred per cent honest. If God wanted me to be ordained, then He would have to take me as I really was. 'Awful,' I said, 'I am really struggling at the moment. When I was first converted just over a year ago prayer seemed really easy and natural, now it seems miles more difficult.' His comment was profoundly reassuring and thought-provoking: 'That appears to be a normal pattern,' he said. 'God allows prayer to be easy and fulfilling for young Christians but then He withdraws in an attempt to draw us deeper. That is when it begins to get difficult.' The encouragement that gave me to persevere was enormous. It gave me a vision for prayer and the idea that if I pursued it and put energy into it then I would discover new depths. And so I have, though like so many things in the spiritual life it has been a case of two steps forward and one step back.

WHAT IS PRAYER – WHAT ARE WE DOING WHEN WE PRAY?

One of the classic works on prayer is a book written in the 1940s by a Norwegian, Ole Hallesby, entitled simply *Prayer*. He opens his book with the quotation from Revelation 3:20:

> 'Behold, I stand at the door and knock: if anyone hears my voice, and opens the door, I will come in and eat with him, and he with me.'

He then goes on:

> I doubt if I know of a passage in the whole Bible which throws greater light on prayer than this one does. It is, it seems to me, the key which opens the door into the holy and blessed realm of prayer. To pray is to let Jesus come into our hearts.'[2]

If we are helping people to pray, if we are helping people to let Jesus come into their hearts, then we are working on their conversion.

SO HOW CAN WE HELP PEOPLE TO PRAY?

The term 'Spiritual Director' is off-putting and makes it sound as if you have to be an expert before you can help someone else learn to pray. The key quality needed is honesty. Prayer is a very personal subject. If faith is personal then prayer which is at the very heart of faith is the most personal dimension of all. It is when talking about our prayer life that we will feel most inadequate. If reading the lesson in church is nerve-racking, doing the intercessions is for some unthinkable. For someone to talk about their own prayer life with you will almost certainly be difficult, but this does not prevent prayer as a topic from being useful in evangelism. Rather than getting them to talk about *their* prayer life start by talking about your own. They will almost certainly be fascinated, they will probably be encouraged as they hear about answers you have received to prayer. They will be stimulated as you relate new discoveries in your prayer style, and they will be reassured when you share the difficulties and disappointments you have experienced. But be warned, only talk about your prayer life if you are prepared to talk about it honestly and fully, sharing both the good and the bad, the down-sides as well as the encouragements. If you talk only about the positive side to prayer you run the risk of making people feel even more inadequate. If you share only the difficulties you will not be giving them anything to aim for.

Adrian Plass in one of his books highlights the fact that in so much Christian literature we hear only the positive things, the stories of answered prayer and miraculous intervention. No one seems to own up to the hassles, the negatives. In *The Sacred Diary of Adrian Plass Aged 37¼* – the hero buys a book on evangelism called *Prayers, Principles, Practices and*

Probable Problems for Precinct Preachers, by A. P. Lunchington. He describes it as follows:

'Sat down with Lunchington's book this evening hoping to pick up a few good tips. What an amazing book. I don't know how the man finds time to eat or sleep. His life is literally one long succession of extraordinary miracles. Everyone he meets and everything he does could have come straight out of the New Testament. In fact the New Testament seems like an early and rather poor rehearsal for Lunchington's life. The man doesn't know what it is to experience doubt or depression, or failure, or discouragement. Everyone he meets seems to get converted and absolutely nothing seems to get him down.'[3]

Men like the fictitious A. P. Lunchington are not human which is why, despite all the supposedly encouraging success stories in his book, the book, far from being helpful, actually serves to increase Plass' feelings of inadequacy. In prayer as in every aspect of our lives we need to be real and to apply the principles outlined in chapter 6 above.

During my training for the ministry in Oxford, I agreed to help on a mission at St Hilda's College. This involved taking part in a discussion with students who had been invited to come and air their questions and difficulties about the Christian faith. On one particular afternoon I ended up being interrogated by one girl who literally barraged me with questions about my prayer life for one whole hour. Like so many people who are quite near to discovering the reality of faith she was fighting hard against it, and came across as quite hostile with her very intelligent and perceptive questions. Once again I had decided to be completely honest and upfront with her, and though I talked of occasions when prayers had been answered, sometimes strikingly so, I also had to admit under her cross-examination that lots of my prayers had not been answered; that I didn't understand why; that although I spent time listening, more frequently than not I didn't hear God saying anything; and that quite a lot of the time praying did seem like sitting by myself in an empty room talking to the walls. As I walked home I felt quite depressed. My description was hardly an advertising agent's idea of how to sell something, and did not seem at all likely to encourage anyone, especially that girl, to have a go at praying. I felt quite convinced that after that sort of description of my prayer life she would write off praying and the Christian faith in general as a complete waste of time. But I was wrong. Two weeks later I found out that the girl had been impressed with my honesty and far from coming to negative conclusions about praying she had continued her exploration into the Christian faith.

LEARNING BY DOING

I have recently returned from Melksham where we had an exceptional weekend in preparation for a mission to take place next year. We had been asked to lead some workshops on prayer. The reason it was a success was because the workshops lived up to their name. Instead of just being talk shops we actually got down and did some praying and some listening. Getting down and doing it together was the key.

We need to help people to find out how to pray. To be spiritual directors or guides for those numerous people who do pray and who are open enough to admit it to us. So how can we help them? Put crudely, our help or guidance can take two forms; firstly, telling them about prayer, giving them ideas that they can then try out on their own. Secondly, doing it with them so that we learn to pray together. The latter will be extremely daunting to some but is a method that will reap double dividends, for if you are prepared to be sensitive and patient then you cannot fail to learn as well as to teach. We need to provide people with opportunities to pray. In our rat-race world finding time to pray on our own is difficult. My wife Lucy and I have a two-and-a-half-year-old son and a four-week-old daughter. Having a toddler has meant that my wife has found it increasingly difficult to set aside time for prayer in the way that she did before having children. She missed praying and yet was struggling to find a new routine. A suggestion from Sister Carol, a colleague at Lee Abbey, not only helped fill some of this vacuum but also helped introduce Lucy to a new way of praying. Carol thought that Lucy might like to come and pray *with* her in her room. They would light a candle and pray silently together around it. This is a form of prayer that Lucy had never tried before but which she found enormously soothing and spiritually enlivening, perhaps because of its contrast with the frenetic toddler-filled rest of the day. Quite often it will be praying with others that will maintain us through these difficult phases of life.

Helping people by praying with them can take place at a very simple and mundane level. Quite often, for example, people will say to me: 'Do say a prayer for me', meaning when I have gone home and am praying later on my own or in the church. One way of helping to develop their prayer life is to take this opportunity and to offer to pray *with* them rather than just *for* them. Please note I am suggesting offering, do not insist upon it. In all things spiritual I try to avoid assaulting people, and the idea of someone praying with them will for some be more than they can take at that time. But the need to be sensitive to the small number of very shy people need not prevent us from offering to pray with people. I usually say something along the lines of 'would it be all right if I said a prayer with you now?' I may also add an escape clause following that question with 'Or would you prefer me to say a prayer when I get home?'

If people do allow you to pray with them do not underestimate just how much one prayer might stimulate them on their pilgrimage. If you pray in normal English for instance, it may be the first time they have ever heard prayer not couched in 'thee', 'thou' and 'thenceforth' language and it may break some of the inhibitions that we all have about praying. How you address God in your prayer may give them a whole new picture of the person that they are praying to. A simple phrase like 'Loving Heavenly Father' may be a radical alternative to someone who would normally begin their prayers 'Almighty God' and may play a vital part in developing their relationship with God. Never underestimate the importance of these tiny details, for it is these minutiae that are really influential in helping people on their journey.

PERSONALITY AND STYLES OF PRAYING

Just as we need to find the appropriate thread of Good News to share with each person we meet, we need also to find the appropriate style of prayer for them. Different people pray differently. If we are to help others to pray we must begin by recognizing that the way they pray will depend on the sort of person they are. The friend who gave my wife her first Bible wrote in it; 'God made us all individuals, don't let us die copies.' We need to remember this, especially when it comes to ways of praying. Recently there has been a spate of published material concerned with the effect of personality.[4] This analysis of personality can be applied to prayer to suggest suitable prayer styles for each personality type. Ruth Fowke for example has written recently on *Personality and Prayer*[5] basing her analysis on Jungian personality types.

I am not suggesting that we need to psychoanalyze each of our friends before offering them any guidance on prayer. Nor do I think it is helpful to pigeon-hole people by giving them labels as to which particular personality type they fit into. People are fluid and cannot be fitted perfectly into any single scheme. However, it is helpful to be aware of the different types of personality because it may make us more sensitive in any suggestions we make about styles and approaches to prayer. As Ruth Fowke puts it

> a prayer pattern that suits people of one personality type may not be suitable for those of a quite different personality, with the result that when new Christians are introduced to an incompatible prayer model, and if it is the only model readily available to them, they may become discouraged and perhaps give up all attempts at developing a prayer life at all.[6]

A Look at the different types of Personality

We shall use Jung's model, even though it is not the only one, largely because it has been recently made popular and accessible by the work of Catherine Briggs and her daughter Isobel Myers who have refined it and produced the 'Myers-Briggs Type Indicator'.[7] Jung divides people up in two ways; firstly, into either extroverts or introverts. Extroverts are people who are re-energized by contact with other people, who go out to meet others; introverts are drained by other people and need space apart from them in order to regain their equilibrium – they turn inwards to re-energize. But there is more to it than that. Extroverts tend to think on their feet, developing their ideas in the process of talking. One of my colleagues here would fit that description. It used to be said of him that 'he wrote his talks after he gave them'! In contrast, introverts need time to think before they can put their thoughts into words. These different characteristics will obviously influence their methods of praying. Ruth Fowke points out, for example, that while extroverts are likely to become long-winded while participating readily in spontaneous extempore prayer, introverts may need to be encouraged to take part at all.

I remember a woman called Betty who belonged to a home-group in the first church I ever attended. She was a highly intelligent and perceptive member of the group and frequently wrote to the vicar asking him questions that arose from her daily Bible readings. She had a good job, could be articulate at times, but she was the odd one out in our prayer group. She was the only one who never prayed out loud, not that there was any pressure to do so. I had long given up the idea that she would ever pray publicly. I can still remember the evening in the middle of our prayer time when she did. I remember opening my eyes, I was so surprised, and I caught sight out of the corner of my eye of the tiny slip of paper she held in her hand on which she had written out her prayer in shorthand. A terrible case of injustice against a women in Pakistan had so gripped Betty's imagination that she felt that she simply must pray – but it was that slip of paper that had given her the confidence to do so. From that time on she prayed regularly but always with a slip of paper. I thank God for her prayers. For introverts like Betty, who are by nature private people, it may be worth encouraging them to do what comes naturally and to listen more than they speak. They may be assisted in prayer that is contemplative and reflective, waiting on God silently in preference to a noisy and verbose style of praying. For extroverts on the other hand it may be more helpful to pray with other people, after all extroverts get their inspiration by feeding on the energy that others provide.

These simple insights into extrovert and introvert personality can help guide us in how to assist people in their prayer. But Jung's analysis does not stop here. Jung further divided extroverts and introverts into four categories, making eight personality types in all. These four categories depend on the way you approach life:

1) Sensing people (experience life primarily through the five senses).
2) Thinking people (experience life primarily through the rational mind).
3) Feeling people (experience life primarily through their emotions).
4) Intuitive people (experience life primarily by relying on their guts/intuition).

Let us look at each in turn.

1 Sensing People

It is obvious that since these people experience life via their senses, they need to use the senses of sight, sound, touch, smell and taste in their prayer life. For these people it is essential to hear or make music, to see visible pictures, a lighted candle or a fresh and fragrant blossom as well as the written word to take them to the living word.[8]

Some of the truth of this I discovered by accident when after struggling with prayer during a difficult period I eventually gave up and went across the room and twiddled on the guitar. I found it relaxed me instantly and I offered up these tunes I composed to God (I certainly wouldn't offer them to a publisher) as an expression of my feelings. Once I had overcome my guilt and persuaded myself that this was allowed I was liberated into a new dimension of prayer. I was further helped in this process of liberation when I stumbled across a marvellous book called *The Spiritual Exercise Book*, by Una Kroll.[9] *The Spiritual Exercise Book* is a highly imaginative daily discipline for two months of prayer. In it Una Kroll concentrates on posture (very important for sensing people) and concrete, tangible forms in prayer as well as meditation on the Bible. Using it greatly enriched my prayer life.

2 Thinkers

These people live predominantly in their minds, reasoning everything through analytically and objectively, and they will like order in their prayer life just as much as they do in their daily work. A disciplined, regular, orderly approach to prayer, both public and private, will most suit this type of person:

For the thinker intelligibility in church services will be important, he will want to hear what is said and understand what's done. He will value well-thought-out preaching . . . many of this type would be helped by writing out short

91

prayers based on their reflections and on their understanding of their faith and to use these prayers constantly in private devotion. Meditation on the prayers of the liturgy should help their worship. The Anglican Church caters well on the whole for this type.[10]

This is the sort of person who criticizes choruses when they are repeated and who is wary of emotion. They may need to be challenged to include their emotional dimension and to get out of their heads and into their hearts. But equally we need to respect the positive side of their reason and what it has to contribute to their prayer life. Thinkers don't always get on brilliantly with the next personality type, whom they have a tendency to look down on.

3 Feelers

In contrast to the preceding group these people are guided by their hearts, not by their heads, putting feelings above logic or reason. It is not that they are unconcerned with facts, rather that they look at whether a fact is good or bad instead of concentrating on whether it is true or false. These are the people who like sermons aimed at the heart and who

> are readily drawn to affective prayer and find it easy and natural to express praise, penitence, gratitude, trust or love.[11]

They see the aim of prayer as intimacy, which may lead to disillusionment when unable to feel the presence of God. Some may run away from facing unpleasant feelings and will need help and encouragement to go through the difficult times, facing rather than avoiding them in order to learn from them.

Although this type may sound egocentric because they are motivated by feelings, intercessory prayer for others will often have a high priority because they will be easily moved by what is affecting other people. Where this personality type will need help is in turning prayer into action; they may be easily moved, but not always moved to act! These people provide a very good balance to the cold, analytical thinker described in the personality type above. Perhaps a balance between the two should be sought within each of us!

4 Intuitives

These are the people who go with their guts and rely predominantly on inspiration. Variety in prayer will be vital for this type, which should come easily, since much of their prayer will be formed in response to all that is going on around them making the act of living into prayer. Christopher Bryant describes their prayer style:

> For the extrovert intuitive prayer will be closely linked to the service of God in the world. If he is a man of faith he will tend to see prayer as co-operating with God in the transformation of the world. It will be natural for him to rely on divine guidance in his planning and deciding. Prayer will indeed be for him the inspiration of action. If the extrovert intuitive is drawn to the service of God in the world, the introvert intuitive is drawn to seek God within himself. He readily sees the truth of what the old spiritual guides affirm, that God is to be found within, in the soul's centre. A contemplative kind of prayer will be normal for him.[12]

A colleague of mine has a motto: 'Pray as you can, not as you can't'. If we are to help people to deepen their prayer life, and ultimately to deepen their relationship with God, we must help them discover ways of praying that suit them. We must help them persevere through the difficult times when prayer seems impossible. And most of all we must remember that prayer is supposed to be fun:

What I wanted most to say is that God is a God of the possible, that the blundering and partial character of our efforts does not surprise or dismay Him. It surprises and dismays us; He works out the details of the friendship not in spite of, but within and because of, our ability to bungle. If our shirts are a bit too stuffed, He is ready to remove some of the padding, and we would do better to smile than to construct a tragedy out of it. He is waiting for us to catch on. He is a God who laughs.[13]

ONE STEP AT A TIME

The aim of evangelism is conversion. But the routes by which people are converted are numerous, and the time taken to journey along the road varies enormously from one person to another. Nor is the journey complete once we are converted. John Finney's research discovered that conversion can take anything from one day to forty-two years, and that many people in the survey saw it as a process that was continuing rather than something which had finished. To evangelize effectively we must understand what we are hoping for when we talk about conversion, and we must understand the processes which help to bring it about.

Conversion is in some circles a dirty word. I once visited an Anglican Clergy Chapter where I had been invited to talk about the work of Lee Abbey. I explained about my job and started asking them what each of their churches was doing in response to the decade of evangelism, when the Rural Dean interrupted: 'I thought we came to hear about Lee Abbey, NOT to have a discussion on conversion.' From the way he almost spat out the word I could tell it jarred with him, as it does with so many people. By way of reply I introduced him to the definition of conversion given in the 1945 report *'Towards The Conversion of England'*:

The aim of evangelism is conversion. Conversion is the reorientation of life from self to God through Christ Jesus. Conversion may be sudden: a revolutionary experience, like a revealing flash of lightning, which enables the convert to commemorate a spiritual birthday. Or conversion may be gradual: an evolutionary development like the dawn of day, or the miracle of the harvest field. But whether sudden or gradual, it is the birthright of every child of God to be converted, or (in St Paul's phrase) to 'be alive unto God in Jesus Christ our Lord'.[1]

When it comes to 'conversion' people fall into two opposite and extreme positions; either they ignore it as unnecessary, thinking most people are really Christian, and conversion is an unusual experience irrelevant to the vast majority of people. Or at the other extreme some see conversion as the be all and end all of evangelism, without realizing that it represents only one of many steps on the Christian pilgrimage. We need a balanced approach to conversion. We need firstly to realize that the vast majority of people in our nation need to be converted in the sense described above and that we have no right to deny them the opportunity of personally accepting Jesus Christ as Saviour and King, and thereby coming to know God in a personal way. And secondly we must recognize that the means by which people come to conversion, and the pace at which they do so, are infinitely varied, and we must therefore make our evangelism flexible enough to allow people to journey forward at their pace and by their own route. John Finney found that:

Those who evangelize often look for quick results ... The gradual process is the way in which the majority of people discover God and the average time taken is about four years:

models of evangelism which can help people along the pathway are needed.[2]

Evangelism is far more like a marathon than it is like a sprint. If we are to see it through we must choose a pace that can be maintained for the whole distance, and which others can comfortably follow. Patience and perseverance will be needed if we are to see people come through to the finish.

But we must not make the mistake of thinking that our job ends with conversion. Conversion is not the conclusion of the journey but an essential step along the way. This should be obvious from the wording given in the Great Commission:

> Therefore go and make disciples of all nations, baptising them in the name of the Father and of the Son and of the Holy Spirit, and teaching them to obey everything I have commanded you.[3]

We are told to go and make disciples, not just converts, but disciples. A disciple is a 'learner' and this emphasis on people's need to learn and develop their faith is emphasized by the phrase that Matthew used: 'teaching them to obey everything I have commanded you'.[4] What we are aiming to do with people, therefore, is to make them pupils, to start them down the path of learning to follow Jesus. This means that the process of evangelism does not end at conversion. It does not end when you have got people into church and have baptized them. Matthew's command emphasizes that evangelism is in one sense a continuous process. We must carry on teaching people and ensure that their faith develops and grows.

When I was working on a mission recently, with a team from a very evangelical church, I was worried that they might pounce on everyone they met, trying to convert all and sundry without discovering whether they were already converted or if they were ready for converting. In an endeavour to prevent this happening I introduced them to the Engel's Scale (see diagram).[5] This scale, which was originally devised by Professor James Engel, and elaborated on by the late David Watson, puts in diagrammatic form the idea that people are at different stages on their journey. Some are a long way off, being almost totally ignorant of the facts of Christianity, whereas others are very close, understanding both the facts and implications of the Christian faith. I pointed out to my team that in a five-day-long mission, I did not expect to get someone from minus ten to conversion in one go. Rather what I hoped was that for each person we met, the mission week would bring them one step forward on their journey.

The team found the Engel's Scale liberating, and on the next occasion when I visited them the vicar's wife told me she had talked about it with virtually everyone she had met. It was liberating because it meant they needn't feel failures if after talking to people they didn't get converted. It also helped because it gave them a purpose with those who were already Christians. The Engel's Scale doesn't finish at the moment of conversion but carries on just like the Christian journey. People may need just as much help in moving on after their conversion as they did leading up to it.

THE ENGEL'S SCALE

-10   No awareness of the supernatural
 -9   No knowledge of Christianity

-8   Initial awareness of Christianity

-7   Interest in Christianity

-6   Understanding of the basic facts of the Gospel

-5   Grasp of the implications of the Gospel

-4   Positive attitude towards the Gospel

-3   An awareness of the need for Christ

-2   Assessment of the cost of discipleship

-1   Decision – 'I turn to Christ'

A new disciple is born – Matthew 28: 19–20

+1   Evaluation of the decision

+2   Initiation into church

+3   Become part of the process of making others disciples

•   Growth in understanding of the faith

•   Growth in Christian character – the fruit of the spirit

•   Discovery and use of gifts – including gifts of the spirit

•   Christian life style

•   Stewardship of resources

•   Prayer

•   Openness to others

•   Effective sharing of faith and life.

Adapted from David Watson, *I Believe in the Church – Study Guide*, p. 47.

I was grateful for the Engel's Scale and the impact it had on the team because it meant that instead of rushing in with a prepacked message aimed at converting everybody, the team had to listen first in an effort to discover where any given individual was in their journey. Then they had to work out how best to help that person to take one step forward.

The evening after showing the mission team the Engel's Scale and suggesting that our aim was to help everybody to take one step forward, I had an evening off. I sat down to read some of Penelope Leach's book, *Baby And Child*. I have a toddler and was swotting up on how to look after him. I suddenly realized that the section which was talking about play could be applied exactly to what I had been saying the previous night about evangelism – if you substitute the word 'journey' for 'play' it describes our job as evangelists perfectly;

> Your toddler wants to be near you as he plays and often he will welcome your help and participation in what he does, but he does not need or want to be told what to do. His play is exploration, discovery and experiment. If you insist on showing him the 'right' way to do things and telling him the answers to questions he has barely formulated, you will spoil the whole process. The art of joining in a toddler's play is to let him be play leader. Provided your dignity will allow you to take this subordinate role you can enrich his play enormously.[6]

For effective evangelism to take place we need to create this sort of environment. We need to surround people with loving and supportive companions as they journey through life:

> Those making the journey of faith need people with whom they can identify. Very few of those we asked made a solitary journey – there were nearly always others around them . . .[7]

To fit this role of companion we need to be similar but different. We need to be close enough for the other person to identify with us, but sufficiently different to challenge them to grow and to change; 'Friends seem to be effective when they are examples of two things – faith and normality.'[8] We must join with people in a journey of exploration, but we must recognize that it is **their** journey and we are called to be helpers, not leaders, to walk alongside, not in front, to contribute but not to control. If we can do this, then we will enrich their journey enormously and at the same time we ourselves will be enriched. Again it is mostly a question of sharing ourselves as we journey together.

One of the greatest privileges in my work travelling around and helping churches in mission is that I have been able to share in part of their journey. One of the most painful things can be saying goodbye. Sometimes ending an involvement with a church after two or three years can be quite a wrench. I remember a church in Essex and the last morning I spent with them:

'The time has come for us to say goodbye,' I said, looking round the room at the faces I had got to know over the previous three years. 'Thank you for the privilege of allowing us to journey with you and to learn from you en route. We have come a long way together and a lot has changed over the last two-and-a-half years.' And indeed it had. I had worked with St Paul's church in Great Baddow for nearly three-and-a-half years (if we include all the planning) on the project to renew and revitalize the life of the church in this town near Chelmsford. The project had been officially launched on 28 October 1990 – a day that I will never forget although I wasn't at the launch. It was the day my first, child, Edward, was born. A momentous day for me as I witnessed a birth and welcomed an event that meant my life would never be the same again. A day equally momentous for St Paul's church as the project was born and the people entered a new era welcoming a process that would leave them changed.

Looking back that morning as I surveyed the sea of faces I thought back to the little vulnerable baby boy who had so needed the care and nurture of his mother and who could now walk and talk and was relishing the first joys of independence. And I thought of the church which we had helped nurture at first protectively, as we helped it take its first faltering steps to renewal – a church that was now weaned and had outgrown the need for my team and the input we gave. I thought back to the first weekend that we had run on the subject of prayer and looking round spotted the couple who on that weekend had given up a golf lesson (shocking for me as a keen golfer) in order to be able to take part in the workshop on the Saturday morning. A couple who were even keener to learn how to pray than they were to learn how to swing a golf club. I smiled, for that had been so encouraging to me on that very first weekend and over the two years I had got to know and like them, and I was going to miss them. I thought back to the training weekend we had run some six months later at the church, giving some basic teaching and exercises about evangelism, and looked over to Derek, one of my team who had helped me with the teaching. I had enjoyed being able to share the workload with him, learning from a course he had written for his home church some of which he used here at St Paul's. It seemed a shame that our partnership in teaching people how to share the Gospel was about to come to an end, I would miss working with him.

I looked back to the hectic five days in March 1992 that made up the focal point of the project, five days of small evangelistic events in people's homes and schools, not to mention the pub, and also some larger events. The notable social evenings we'd had when the church had ordered 140 portions of fish and chips (not to mention a few sausages for the children and pizzas for any vegetarians); evenings when we did Israeli dancing and silly games. It was a week the church had called

'Voyages of Discovery', a title which emphasized the theme of journeying together to find out more about the Christian faith. I thought of the team that had come with me then, one of whom was now back in her native Poland; we too had journeyed on.

And now we were at the end of what we had called the Follow-up Weekend. We had returned for one final visit to hear how things had been going since that mission week in March and to help them to reflect on it. We had asked everyone to cast their minds back and tell us what they had remembered – what had made an impression upon them. All the answers they gave were different but again and again it was the fun, the liveliness and most of all the people that had made the deepest impression. People had been encouraged and together we had moved on in our pilgrimage.

I asked them all to sit in silence and to think about how they had changed during the course of the past two years, to try and think how they had moved on. I gave them a couple of minutes and then asked them to think who had helped them to take a step forward in their faith, who had encouraged them, or taught them or given them some practical help. I wanted to know who was it that had supported them in their journey. Then I asked them to do something really difficult. I pointed out how often in church life we hear criticism and how seldom we hear encouragement. 'Wouldn't it be great if we could encourage those people who had helped us in our journey. What I'd like you to do is to tell us all as a group if you wish (and only if you wish) who it is that has helped you; and if they are here today to thank them.' There was a pause while I listened to my heart beating more quickly than usual. I was terrified that either no-one would speak at all or that they would simply thank me as the speaker and leader of the team which would be hideously embarrassing. I needn't have worried, no one thanked me, though they did thank the team as a whole. But I sat there deeply moved as slowly and nervously they thanked each other. Several thanked the vicar for the part he had played in aiding them on their journey. It must have been a bit embarrassing for him sitting there listening to the gratitude of his flock expressed publicly and openly, but I thought it was well worth it for the encouragement that it must have given him.

We then looked at what had happened since our last visit. Some new events had occurred, open-air carol singing had taken place in order to follow up an open-air singing event we had done during the mission week, during which we had handed out invitations outside the Co-op to come to the Sunday services. Individuals commented how the mission week had brought dividends in talking about their faith in their daily lives. Someone commented how after a quiz evening they now found it easier to talk about their faith with the friends they had brought along that night. One man told us how he had given his testimony at work, something he had never done before. The vicar then outlined plans for the future – a series of social events; a questionnaire which they were going to take round some of the houses and a town-wide festival of faith with the other churches in Great Baddow to take place in the coming year.

This final weekend reflecting and looking back on the mission and how people had changed as a result of it had been profoundly encouraging for both the church and for me because its effects had been long lasting. 'Before we finish,' I said, 'there is one more thing I want you to do. I want you to draw on a large piece of paper a foot and a hand.' They looked puzzled but had got used to the sort of teaching methods I used by now and set to drawing as best they could a foot and a hand. Several drew round their shoes to get the shape, some put their hands on paper and then drew round their fingers. Even so we had several feet with four or even six toes. When they had all finished I explained what I wanted them to do. 'Write down in your foot what you think is the next step forward for you on your Christian journey.' When they had done that I went on: 'In the hand, please write down the name of the person whose help you think you will need in order to make that step. The person whose hand you will be able to hold in order to take that step.' When they had all finished I explained what I wanted them to do with their feet and their hands. 'I want you to bring your foot up here and to lay it in front of the altar as an act of dedication to God and as you stand there pray, asking God to help you.' They came up in twos and threes and did as I had asked while the rest of us sat in silence and joined our prayers with theirs. 'Finally,' I said, 'go and show the hand to whoever's name is written on it, tell them the step that you want to take and ask them for their help; be brave, ask and I believe that you will receive.' I had been worried that some people might see this exercise as patronizing, a bit like treating them as children, but I was reassured the next day at the final service when numbers of people from the congregation who had been unable to attend the workshop on the Saturday came up and asked if they could please have a foot to write down their next step. I quickly got one of my team to draw a foot on several pieces of paper and he stood at the back at the end of the service as people walked out giving them that foot. It seemed so appropriate as they stepped out at this parting of the ways for them to be thinking of that one step more.

CHURCH – THE FINAL
FRONTIER

On one of our mission projects, my wife Lucy had taken part in
a youth event aimed at bringing in outsiders. The rooms used
for the meeting adjoined the church. At the end of the evening
Lucy and two teenagers who were reluctant to go home discovered that the exit had been locked and the only way out was
through the church. It was late and Lucy was eager to get
home, but the two youngsters did not hurry. They wandered off
into the semi-dark depths of the building. 'Is this a church?'
asked one in amazement. 'What's this?' said the other as he
stood by the altar. Quite obviously they had never set foot in
church before.

To the majority of people in this country, church seems like
another planet. We are just worlds apart culturally when it
comes to comparing Christian culture and normal culture. We
have as much chance of persuading some people to come to
church as we have of getting them to fly to the moon. To many
people, the church threshold is simply too big to get across.
Growing numbers of people are brought up with almost nil
experience of church. They are never taken by parents, not
baptised, and certainly not sent to Sunday school. With
increasing numbers of people living together, or opting for
register office weddings, and with more and more funerals
taking place at the crematorium, the opportunities for meeting

people on the three occasions when the church 'hatches, matches and dispatches', are becoming rarer. For some people church remains a foreign world.

People are very unlikely to venture into places where they fear they might be embarrassed. And one potential source of embarrassment is not knowing the acceptable norms of behaviour. I remember how intimidated I felt when I first took up golf, because I did not know the correct form. Where did I change my shoes, was I allowed to bring my clubs into the changing room, what was the standard of dress required to go into the bar (it varied at different times of day), and what on earth was a spike or stud bar? The only reason I overcame this hurdle was because I was absolutely determined to play golf, and because I had a friend who took me in tow and I followed. For most people, entering a church is to enter a world far more complex and foreign than entering a golf club. For some people it is probably on a par with you or I entering a Buddhist temple. Imagine going to a service on your own in a Buddhist or Sikh temple. What do you have to wear? Do you have to take your shoes off? Where do you sit, and what posture do you adopt? Who does what? And what are you expected to do by way of participation?

Acceptable patterns of behaviour vary greatly even between the different Christian denominations. We took a Roman Catholic to our Anglican church recently. Poor chap, every time the vicar said, 'Let us pray,' he stood up, quite normal in his Roman Catholic church, while every Anglican immediately dived to their knees.

Try to imagine for a moment what it is like to be a complete newcomer to a church. Once you have succeeded in crossing the threshold of a church, you are handed a huge pile of hymn books, prayer books, and notice sheets. First you have to find a place to sit, and then find your way round the service, without making it too obvious that you are trying to see the page number (always in tiny print) in the prayer book of the person next to you. And to survive a service of Holy Communion, you have to know when to go forward and what posture to adopt at the rails, and which route to take back to your seat, which is often different from the route up. A vicar told me recently of a woman who had started attending services they held in a local school. She had never been to a service of Holy Communion before. When everyone else went forward, in order not to be conspicuous, she too went to the front and in her turn was handed a piece of bread. Not knowing what to do with it, she put it in her pocket. She managed to drink from the cup as that was proffered to her lips. After the service she had the courage to go up to the person who had led it, and said, 'Tell me, why did you give me a piece of bread when I came forward?' Perhaps the saddest part of the story is the man did not know what to say in reply.

There are many people for whom the form of our services is a total mystery. If we are to succeed in reaching these people with the Good News about Jesus, then we have to be aware just how huge a hurdle it is to come to church. One useful exercise to raise our awareness is to invite somebody you know, who has never been to church, and ask them to walk into the building from the outside and to make observations for you. The eyes of a stranger will spot many things that have become so familiar to you that you fail to notice them. Ask them to make comments on the appearance of the building, the noticeboard, the entrance, the welcome, and indeed the whole of the service if you can persuade them to come to one. Their observations may open up our eyes, as to what it feels like to be a stranger coming in from the outside.

Once we have become aware just how difficult it is for some

people to come into church, we must do several things. We must first of all stop waiting for them to come in of their own accord. We must go out to them and help them to cross the threshold. Waiting for people to come unprompted and unaided into our churches is like waiting for fish to jump out of the sea and onto hooks suspended some distance above the water. When I was little and went trout fishing, one trout did jump into our boat, but I would not wait around for it to happen again.

Oddly enough when fish do jump into our net some churches seem determined to do their best to throw them out again. I am referring to the strict policy adopted by some churches on the baptism of children. Many people who never come to church approach the Church of England to get their children christened. This represents one of the greatest opportunities for evangelism offered to the Anglican Church. But many churches instead of viewing it positively react in a way that serves to drive these people away from church. Some churches take an exclusive attitude reserving baptism for the in-group of churchgoers. Given the strong statements and promises made in the baptism service by the parents and godparents, this is at first sight understandable. But it is based on a misunderstanding of the way the majority of people come to faith. People do not find faith and then come to church, it is the other way round. Belonging precedes believing. John Finney suggested that

> 'Whatever the theological implications the evidence suggests that in practice parents need to be shown total welcome and also a way in which they can find out more about God in their own time.'[1]

Many people who ask for their children to be baptised will not understand the promises, let alone believe them. But, instead of excluding them from the church because of this, we should use baptism as a means of helping them to belong to the church. The reason the font is normally placed near the door of the church is to emphasize that baptism is equivalent to entry into the church family. Baptism is about belonging. We must help people to belong even if they have very hazy beliefs, in the hope that by belonging they may become believers.

This does not mean that we treat the promises made in the baptism lightly. I believe a successful approach, that is not exclusive, can be found. When I was a curate our church did have quite a strict baptism policy and we were quite rigorous in the demands we made of the people who came to us for baptism. One day I received a telephone call from my little sister Jill, who at this time was not a churchgoer. 'I'm ringing to ask if you would be kind enough to baptize Tom.' My instant reaction was that if I was to have any integrity I could not show any favouritism to a member of my own family. I must treat her in the same way I would treat one of my own parishioners. This meant spelling out the meaning and obligations of baptism. But I wanted to be positive not negative. 'I would love to baptize Tom,' I replied. 'But before I agree to do so I want to talk through the baptism service with you. It contains a number of promises, and I want to make sure that you are happy with the things you have to say.'

Because we were unable to get together for a while, I sent my sister a copy of the baptism service and explained what was involved and what she and her husband would have to say. In particular I pointed out that they were committing themselves to bringing Tom up within the Christian family which meant regular attendance at their local church. We then arranged to meet at our father's house and talk it through. I must admit that I was dreading the meeting. Partly because I thought that if we decided not to go ahead with the service my father would never understand. After a delicious Sunday lunch we sat down to talk about it. My sister's husband Trevor opened the conversation: 'We've thought about it and we agree with you.' Great, I thought, but just what bit are they agreeing with? I asked him to elaborate. 'We want to postpone the baptism until we have settled into a church. We'll be moving house in the next couple of months. Once we've done that we'll start going along to church and then we'll fix the baptism.' And that is exactly what they did. They started attending the Family Service, and then my sister went along to the Pram Service where she met other mums. By that time they'd had a second child and I baptized both Tom and Jonathan in their local church in Westbury.

How much did Jill and Trevor understand the promises they made? Only partially – it takes time for the meaning of something like 'I turn to Christ' to really sink in. But I do not believe in setting a doctrine exam for those who come for baptism. I was more than happy to baptize their children despite their hazy understanding of the Christian faith, because they had begun the journey, and because they now belonged to the Church. I felt confident that God would deepen their faith as they walked slowly forward. And He did. Tiny things like participating in a Crib Service where they carried up a camel all played their part in their developing faith. Two years later both my sister and her husband are on the Confirmation Course. What is more, Jill is playing her part in helping others to come into the Church.

In the parish church she attends in Westbury they have a system of allocating 'Friends' to everyone who brings a child to be baptized. My sister is one of these baptism 'Friends'. The job of a baptism Friend is to attend the baptism and call a few days later to deliver the baptism certificate which quite deliberately is not given out at the service. Still later the 'Friend' visits, taking a copy of the parish magazine in which the child's baptism is announced. Then they visit and invite the mother along to the Pram Service, which is called 'First Steps to Worship'. If the person is interested then the 'Friend' arranges to meet her so they can go along together. So simple but so profoundly effective in helping people with little experience of worship to come into the Church.

We need to make our churches as 'user-friendly' as possible. We need to think through every detail, so that it becomes as easy as possible for an outsider, who has never been to church before, to come into our building, to participate, and to understand what is going on in our services. We must look closely at how we welcome people, how they find a seat, how they follow the service – the giving out of page numbers and readings in our services must be such as to make them accessible, whilst avoiding sliding into the mundane and banal. Services must be easy to follow, without suffering the loss of dignity or mystery. The balance is difficult to achieve and requires a great deal of thought and preparation and detailed planning, but it is a priority.

Considerable discussion has taken place recently about making church suitable for non-churchgoers. Some of this stems from the spate of 'church planting' which has gone on in recent years. A number of Sunday services now take place in non-church buildings, frequently halls, schools or community centres, which offer an opportunity to 'dechurchify' things. Sadly all too often these 'church plants' have simply made the school or hall look as similar to a church as possible, rather than thinking through what could be done differently given the architectural features.

New impetus in this area has come from the experience of the church in Willow Creek, whose rallying call is to set up 'church for the unchurched'. A number of conferences have now taken place in this country based on the pioneering work that has gone on in the United States of America. Willow Creek argue that the usual Sunday service, while suitable for believers who have become frequent churchgoers, is totally unsuitable for those who neither believe nor usually attend church. They have had the courage to completely redesign what goes on on Sunday mornings, in an effort to attract the previously unchurched to something that allows for a presentation of the Gospel, using familiar idioms. Since this will no longer satisfy the needs of the converted believers, additional worship is offered, aimed at Christians, on a mid-week night. While several questions must remain about the particular model offered by Willow Creek, we must commend the courageous way they have attempted to make church far more accessible to outsiders.

John Finney's research stresses the importance of encountering not just individual Christians but the Christian community as a whole:

> To belong to a group of friends who were Christians was important. For most people the corporate life of the church is a vital element in the process of becoming a Christian and for about a quarter it is the vital factor. Forms of evangelism which fail to recognize this are doomed.[2]

The Christian community itself is evangelistic. Here at the Lee Abbey Community we see our *raison d'être* as being 'The renewal of the Church by lay training and evangelism *through community*'. People will see Jesus in individual Christians that they meet, as I suggested in chapter 6. But equally Jesus should be seen in a group of Christians, in a Christian community. The love that we show one another, the ability to be reconciled and to forgive one another will all communicate the love and character of Jesus Christ. The challenge to churches is to become a Christian community. We must show people how to live together in our increasingly individualistic society. People are crying out for a rediscovery of community.

One of the most popular television soaps begins with a song:

Neighbours, everybody needs good neighbours, with a little understanding you can find the perfect blend. Neighbours should be there for one another, that's when good neighbours become good friends.[3]

It seems strange that the programme is so attractive in an age when increasingly we don't even know the names of those who live next door. Present-day society is increasingly individualistic. We live in nuclear families – with our 2.4 children (I had my second child during the writing of this book, so I am nearly there!) and we live in our house for the most part keeping ourselves to ourselves. We have less and less need to know our neighbours, indeed we have less and less reason to go out at all. The home has become an all-sufficient place where our every need is provided for. We no longer go to the cinema, 90% of homes have their own videos; we no longer need to go and play bridge, chess or even golf with anyone – we can do all that upstairs on our computer. We get in our cars in our interconnecting garages, drive to work, come home and go straight back into our sealed and secure little house. No need to even see our neighbours let alone talk to them. And Jesus said:

Love your neighbour as you love yourself.[4]

In other ways too our culture militates against us getting to know other people. Society is becoming increasingly dehumanized as it becomes more and more automated. Soon we will meet more robots on our daily travels than humans. If you pop along to the tourist information at Lynton Town Hall in sleepy North Devon to discover what is available locally you meet not a smiling face but a television set with instructions to push button 'A' for entertainment, 'B' for beaches and 'E' for eating out. Go into a DIY store outside any large town, try and find somebody to help or advise you and you will have great difficulty; they have dispensed with people in favour of automatic dispensing machines and computerized checkouts. Recently when I went to my local bank and asked the cashier if I could write a cheque out to cash, she looked startled. 'Have you lost your cashpoint card? We prefer you to use the cashpoint machines.' Personally I prefer dealing with humans rather than robots however quick they are. And there lies the clue to our antisocial world – speed. We are in too much of a hurry – no time to stop and chat: 'Must be going' is becoming the automatic second phrase to follow any superficial greeting. 'Hello, sorry, must dash, forgot to pick up the kids/ get to work/catch the shops' (delete as applicable).

So why is the programme 'Neighbours', which portrays a wholly unrealistic and idealistic little neighbourhood around Ramsey Street, so popular? Why is 'Brookside' similarly drawing large viewing figures? Perhaps it is because they both create a world in which people *do* have time for other people, a world where people *do* know the other people living in their street and even count them as their friends.

Perhaps programmes like these tap into the unconscious where deep down the idea of friendship and the need for it still lingers.

And God said it is not right that the man should be alone.[5]

Genesis reminds us that man was created a social animal, no man is an island sufficient unto himself. We were designed to be social – we need one another.

One of the keys to evangelism lies in demonstrating true community living. Perhaps this is one reason that the Church is so ineffectual, because we are so poor at, and we work so little on, our relationships. There are still so-called Christian churches where people do not even know the name of their fellow worshippers; where people come to a service and leave with no contact other than a cursory handshake from the vicar. Churches where the idea of sharing the peace is anathema, where fellowship is nonexistent. Where people if challenged would say their faith was a personal matter and where they succeed in keeping it that way. Such churches can hardly be called Christian, for a Christian church is the church of the reconciled, of people who are reconciled to God *and* to each other. Somebody once said the church should be the place where we cannot live without one another. All too frequently it is the place where we cannot live *with* one another. If John Finney is correct then the single most important task in evangelism is to help people overcome these barriers and form friendships. If it is friends that bring faith then a cynic looking at the decline of the Church might say we are a pretty unfriendly bunch, and he wouldn't be far wrong.

Good relationships do not just happen, they have to be worked at. As a married man of ten years I have learned this the hard way, and regret the lack of schooling in the basic art of making and mending relationships. And it is not just within marriage; in any community friendship is fragile. A Christian community is no different, and the experience of living on the Lee Abbey Christian Community in Devon is a sharp reminder of the pain as well as the pleasure that living in close community with a family of seventy brings. As a regular feature of community life we have talks and discussions about forming community and I lead a class on relationships for those who have just joined, and who may in their naivety believe that living with an all-Christian group of people will be a doddle. Our churches need to work at the formation of true community. Scott Peck began his book about the creation of community called *The Different Drum*, with a blunt statement:

In and through community lies the salvation of the world, nothing is more important.[6]

I do not believe that to be an overstatement. And I believe it gives us a great deal to do before effective evangelism can take place. Vincent Donovan was a Roman Catholic priest who went as a missionary to the Masai in East Africa. His approach was to evangelize them not as individuals but as whole communities – clans and tribes. This led him to reflect on the lack of community in America and in the West as a whole and upon the difficulty which that made for evangelism. He describes an occasion when teaching a class of high school students about community. He asked a girl picked at random who would be affected if she committed suicide:

Without thinking another minute she pointed to a friend and said, 'Mary here and my mother.' That was all. No other

117

person in that crowded room, no one else volunteered to say he or she would certainly be affected. The others in fact agreed with her. If that was the limit of her real community, I could not even begin to imagine her life. Neither could I be sure that Christianity would be at all possible for her – or for the others. If she were at all typical of any segment of America, then I should think before anything else. America's greatest need would be first of all to find a sense of community again, or for baptised people, to find community again through Christianity.[7]

We urgently need to rediscover community. In rural Britain where the village shop is disappearing; in urban or suburban landscapes where the shape of community has been eroded so that people do not belong anywhere; and in our inner cities where trust has been driven off the streets by fear. Community is what is called for. And it is the Church that holds the key to the rebuilding of community. The Church that knows how to re-form community and the Church that has to model it for the outside world. The Church in itself must be evangelistic. It must stand as a sign of the Kingdom of God. That means it must point to the realities about which it speaks. The Church stands as evidence that the claims of the Bible are true and that we can begin to experience them here and now in our daily lives. The Church stands as the sign that there is another way to live – and that way is in community. The Church must demonstrate how relationships work; how relationships ought to be once we have discovered that new relationship with our Father. Our relationships within the Church should be such that people looking at the Church from outside will be attracted to come in and discover that ultimate relationship with God as Father.

HOME, THE HALFWAY HOUSE

If your evangelism relies on expecting people to come to church, don't hold your breath. Even allowing for significant progress in making church more user-friendly, church will remain for some people a step too far. To get people from nil contact with church to attending church, in one step, will simply not prove possible. What we therefore need are stepping stones to help them bridge the gap between the normal culture and church culture. Indeed you could describe mission as laying stepping stones down so that 'they can cross over to us' and 'we can cross over to them'.

What is really needed is a halfway meeting point. If the strategy of persuading people or inviting people to come to church is unrealistic, then perhaps we need a two-step strategy; invite them somewhere where they can meet church people and encounter church culture, and where they can acclimatize (and we also acclimatize to them). Then when they are ready we bring them to church proper. Rather like a pressure chamber to allow divers to come to the surface. Carefully and slowly the pressure is made level until quite safely the diver can be reintroduced to our atmosphere. Likewise we need to re-create social opportunities, where outsiders and church can slowly acclimatize themselves to each other in an unpressured environment.

This two-stage approach is what lies behind all social activities (that is not to say that social activities are not good in themselves). Any church worth its salt will be aware that some people will not enter the church building whatever is put on the menu; they therefore organize social events in locations where outsiders will feel comfortable. This may mean avoiding any property owned by the church including church halls and rooms. It is better to use village halls, clubs, the British Legion, pubs – anything that is neutral territory and will be seen as neutral territory by the outsider or non-churchgoer. It should be obvious to anyone sporting, that always requiring people to play an away fixture is simply unfair.

Similarly, expecting 'them' to 'come to us' and meet us on our ground is grossly unfair and unrealistic. We need to venture onto their turf, where we may feel less secure, and in surroundings where they will certainly feel comfortable even if we do not. To succeed in its mission every church needs to have regular occasions held on neutral territory to which outsiders can come and at which they will be put at their ease. This means not only the venue, but also the content of the evening must be attractive and non-threatening. This does not mean it needs to be unchallenging. It is quite possible to organize social evenings which include a thought-provoking and challenging teaser of some sort which will provoke some response in the open-minded. An epilogue at the end of the evening can be fun, light-hearted, creative and artistic, using dance, drama, music, and interviews, whilst still remaining contentful and challenging.

Equally, there will be occasions where the aim will be purely social without any need to have an address of any sort. People dislike being preached at, and for the church to be seen to take a break from preaching or talking at people, and instead to simply enjoy them at a social function, will itself speak volumes. Apart from the fact that we should enjoy this purely social evening for its own sake, it offers a great opportunity for non-churchgoers to mingle with those who attend, and to discover that at least some of those Christians are normal. People's perceptions of churchgoers are often hideously distorted, imagining Christians to be out of date, out of touch, and out of fashion. To many outsiders the idea of a Christian still conjures up an image of someone who does not drink, does not smoke, does not have fun, and really does not live at all!

Social events provide an excellent opportunity of proving that Christians are normal whilst at the same time having something that makes them different. This combination is important: 'Faith only seems to be evangelistically effective when it is allied with similarity in other aspects of life'.[1] People need to be able to identify with Christians yet be sufficiently challenged by the difference that Christ has made to their lives. Perhaps this is what we need when as the Bible puts it, we are challenged to be 'in' the world but not 'of' the world.[2] Social events provide an obvious opportunity for identifying with people. Perhaps we need to be challenged more deeply by the way Jesus was perfectly prepared to go wherever the people were – into the homes of outcasts and sinners without being afraid of losing His uniqueness. We need not be scared that letting our hair down in a village dance or social evening means we are necessarily letting God down. In the present climate, Christians who claim to be joy-filled need to prove that they can enjoy themselves.

The best halfway meeting point is the home. More and more evangelism is taking place in the privacy of people's homes. One method that is tried and tested, in several different areas of the country, is Michael Wooderson's 'Good News Down The

Street'.[3] This strategy incorporates the ultimate away fixture, since it involves going into the person's home. Rather than finding a neutral venue, the church goes all the way into the home of the interested person for a six-week course, explaining the basics of the Christian faith. This approach has been notably successful where people come to church asking for something – baptism or marriage – and the church offers the course as a means of preparation. But it does require some degree of enthusiasm to invite three people into your home for one evening a week, six weeks running. Most people are wary of committing themselves to this, until they are pretty sure what they are letting themselves in for.

Our homes provide the best venue for evangelism. And we need to use our homes in a variety of ways to offer outsiders a stepping stone to faith. The home provides just the right level of intimacy and atmosphere for talking about faith. In a larger social gathering such as in a village hall, the conversation will normally be just a degree more formal, and a little more superficial. The smaller group, the more intimate atmosphere of the home, create an opportunity to talk at a level that is just one degree more personal and more real.

On virtually all of our missions we use people's homes for evangelistic events. The possible permutations are endless but the basic idea is very simple. The hosts invite a number of their friends to come for refreshments plus discussion. Someone other than the host runs the discussion part of the evening where Christianity is the central topic of conversation. It sounds easy, and it really is. Let us look at it in some more detail.

Firstly, we are talking of inviting friends, not strangers. The best people for the hosts to invite are those friends who are used to coming into their home; people who have been before for other purely social events, dinner parties, or who just pop in for coffee. These people will automatically feel relaxed, coming onto what is already familiar territory.

Secondly, the people are invited for refreshments and a discussion about Christianity. The invitation, however it is made, spells out explicitly that part of the evening will be taken up with a discussion about Christianity. There must be no conning of people, getting them there under false pretences. As long as it is put positively, most friends will be interested to come to such a discussion. Of course it does depend on how you ask. 'We're having a Christian thing at our house, I don't suppose you'd like to come', is hardly likely to get a warm response. Whereas 'We're having some friends round for eats and for a discussion about whether Christianity is relevant today. We'd really love you to come', is likely to be well received. It tells them that other people will be there; that there are refreshments; and we rank you amongst our friends and want you to be there. A positive invitation is likely to get a positive result.

For the hosts the inviting is the hard part. Once we have got past the dread of actually asking people to come, apart from worrying whether any will turn up, the job of the host is effectively over. On the evening, the host can leave it to someone else to lead the discussion. Christians are almost phobic in their reaction to inviting friends to Christian events. This is because we presume, usually wrongly, that most people will be hostile or at least negative about the idea of Christianity. When my wife Lucy was at Sussex University, the Christian Union ran a series of discussions. Christian students were encouraged to invite people with whom they shared accommodation. In Lucy's case this meant Lee. Lee was hardly what Lucy considered promising material. A tough cockney, and very bright with it, she feared that he would be very hostile to an invitation to a Christian event. Several times she was on the verge of inviting him but finally chickened out. When Lucy turned up for the discussion group on her own, feeling guilty for not having invited anybody, who should she see sitting there, invited by someone else, but Lee. If only she had had the courage to ask, she would have had the joy of a positive response.

When I was a curate we had about thirty regular Home Groups. The Rector wrote to each home group leader saying he wanted them to hold an evangelistic home meeting to which members of the home group could invite their friends. I well remember the next meeting we had with the home group leaders. Virtually unanimously they were adamant. They couldn't possibly do it. All sorts of dreadful responses were imagined on the part of those who might be invited. Only one woman, Christine, quietly spoke out and said she would have a go with her group. Everyone looked rather disbelieving; the expressions on their faces seeming to say, 'It'll never work'. The next time the home group leaders met she reported back that her group had invited some people who seemed quite interested and who had said that they would come. Two months later, Christine reported that they'd had their evangelistic home meeting, people had come and had enjoyed it, so much so that several had said that they would like to have another such opportunity later in the year. Encouraged by Christine's experience one or two more leaders decided to risk it. Some time after I left the parish I heard that virtually every group had held a meeting, and a number of them were on to their second.

It does take courage to invite people, but instead of assuming that they will be negative about it, we should go in presuming that they will be enthusiastic. After all we enjoy church, so why shouldn't they? If you want to know who to invite then a dangerous strategy if you dare to pursue it is to pray about it. God might put somebody's name or face into your mind. One person who dared to pray, and dared to act on it, was Carole Briggs. I will let her tell her story in her own words:

Some time ago our clergy team decided that each house group should organize an evangelistic supper party. Each member should invite a friend or friends who didn't go to church, lay on a supper and one of the clergy would speak. My heart sank, I thought about it, decided I didn't want to do it and furthermore it wasn't a good idea. Satisfied, I decided to ignore it. My husband was a house group leader and I a sort of assistant. He agreed so we did nothing. Some groups held parties with great success and we had reports at our Sunday evening services. It became more difficult to dismiss the idea, and eventually we thought that if we did one, then we could say we had done ours, and that would have been an end to it. I started praying about who to invite and began to realize that Sue and Mick Whyatt were the people – particularly Sue. My younger daughter had been at primary school with their elder daughter, and Sue and I'd had many talks about Christianity, and 'religion'. Their daughter had wanted to go to Sunday school and we had taken her every Sunday when she was about six to eight years old. Sue and Mick didn't even come to the Christmas meeting when parents were invited to come and see them perform and admire their children's work. Mick had been brought up by parents who were interested in all religions, and had tried all sorts of things – Buddhism, community living, Quakers, and he was very mixed up and wanted to steer clear. When they married, Mick would not be baptized just so that he could be married in an Anglican church, which the vicar said was necessary. He felt that was the wrong reason, so they were married in a register office and were very hurt about it. Sue had been brought up at Sunday school, I think had been confirmed. The last thing I wanted to do was go and ask a couple of people who I had only seen in passing for about the last ten years, but it seemed I had to. So with sinking heart and hoping that they would not be in, I went to call. Sue was in, and I started by saying, 'I wanted to invite you to dinner but there is a catch!' She fairly quickly said she would come and then telephoned to say Mick would too. I was amazed, later Sue said that she realized that it was an invitation she had been waiting for, for fifteen years. Sue realized the hurt over the wedding was a wall that she had built, and when Geoffrey and Lucy talked about sitting on the fence, that's just what she felt she was doing. The next day she came to church and Mick came spasmodically for ten months and was confirmed about a year later! This year Mick was on the Parochial Church Council.

The evenings we organized during my curacy were billed in terms of 'Come and hear one of the clergy talking about what faith means to them'. But it doesn't need to be a 'professional' vicar. The best discussion evenings flow from ordinary Christians, telling their ordinary stories. The formula could not be more simple. If I am leading the evening, when the refreshments are over, we call everyone to order and get them to sit in as near a circle as possible. After thanking the host for providing coffee, and for opening their home, I explain that the aim of the evening is to have a discussion about Christianity. I tell them that the emphasis is on discussion and not monologue, and that I hope that they will join in but nobody will be forced to do so. I then set a time limit for the discussion, explaining that however lively the discussion is, we will pause in an hour and that anyone who wants to can go from that point on. But I mention that there will be more coffee and anyone who wishes to stay and carry on is welcome to do so.

To get the discussion going I introduce two Christians and get each of them to give a five-minute 'nugget' from their Christian journey. It might be about their conversion, or an answer to prayer, or a difficult patch. Then we simply throw it open for discussion. At this point I usually use a joke I picked up from Barry Kissell; 'There's often silence at this point which is good because it shows that you are thinking, but if it goes on too long, it makes me nervous!'. I have never led an evening where we have failed to have a lively discussion, more frequently the difficulty is to get people to stop talking, rather than getting them started.

I well remember the evening of Dennis Egett's evangelistic home-meeting. It gave my wife hysterics – literally. Dennis Egett was a retired man in his seventies who told me he had invited his neighbours who were all elderly. I was going round to lead the discussion scheduled to start at seven-thirty and to last an hour, followed by coffee for anyone who wanted to stay. I told my wife Lucy that I would be home at around nine-thirty, ten o'clock at the latest, and that I would walk home across Ashtead Park. At eleven-thirty, when I had still not returned home, she tried to find the Egetts' phone number, but discovered it was ex-directory. So she drove round at a quarter to midnight to find the house in darkness with no cars outside. In tears, thinking I had been mugged on my way home she was ringing the rector, just as I walked in at five past midnight. We had been in rooms at the back of the house, hence no lights, and there were no cars because all of the neighbours had walked. But the discussion had gone on right up to midnight, because, despite their age, the people so valued the opportunity to talk about one of the things that is normally taboo, religion.

It seems to me that people are longing to have an opportunity to talk about religion, and that the comfort and intimacy of a home creates just the right atmosphere. The variations on a theme to get the discussion started are endless, as are the titles that can be used to advertise them: 'Grill a Christian'; 'What do you expect of the Church?'; 'Your family and how to survive it'; 'What happens when you die? – God knows!' We've had groups for men and groups for women. One time we even had a bread-making demonstration followed by a discussion based around Jesus' claim to be the bread of life and the meaning of Holy Communion. The possibilities are limitless. But whatever means is used to get the evening going, it is discussion that is the key. And it is vital to allow people to create and to follow their own agenda rather than set it for them. The most important thing is to allow people to have their say and not to feel you need to answer everything that comes up. I remember being told by Barry Kissell after the first ever home meeting I attended that frequently when people have been allowed to air their objections to the Christian faith, the objections simply fade away. We must respect people, what they think and their beliefs. I always say in my introduction to the evening that I want to hear their views, and I want the opportunity to say what I believe. I don't want to ram my belief down anybody's throat, but I do want to give people something to think about.

After the hour of discussion is up, I get the host to bring more coffee. But before I do so I always sum up the evening, and formally give them some way of continuing an investigation into Christian things. This may mean advertising a course, or offering a booklet. Sometimes we hand out follow-up cards, which people can fill in indicating whether they would like a free copy of a gospel, or a visit from someone in order to talk further. If the church has regular home group meetings, then whether or not they are on the basics of the faith, I advertise these. I would suggest that if people had enjoyed the evening's discussion they might like to join a more regular forum. In this way the evangelistic home meeting can act as a taster for a more regular discussion group.

It is over the coffee, when the more formal discussion is over, that the most positive conversations usually begin. Although the discussion may carry on as before in one large group, more often the group fragments, so that several small groups discuss issues of particular interest to individuals. This means that the Christians need to be positioned evenly around the room rather than in one block, so that each can take part in a different conversation. Thinking through the detail is especially important if you want the evening to go smoothly and have the minimum of interruptions.

For meetings in the home to work effectively, the home must be inviting. People coming into our homes need to feel safe and unthreatened. This has far more to do with the ethos than with the decor. Warmth coming from the hosts is far more important than that coming from the central heating. Our homes themselves should be evangelistic, so that anyone who enters feels a warmth and a welcome that reflects God's accept-ance and welcome for them. Our home should be a place where people encounter love. This cannot be manufactured, but there are things that you can do to help the process. Some homes on our community at Lee Abbey are places where people are always popping in and coming to stay, whilst others are less easy to penetrate. If you want to succeed in making people come to an evangelistic supper party, but they have never been in your home before, then I recommend that before having the evangelistic event you invite them for something purely social. Apart from putting them at their ease and introducing them to some of your friends, it will make them feel less 'got at' if they are invited to non-Christian events too. Invite them over for dinner or coffee, whichever is natural in the culture in which you live. Barbecues in summer, Guy Fawkes bonfire nights, or mince pie and sherry parties at Christmas, all provide great excuses to get the neighbours over.

When we did a mission in Kenilworth in Warwickshire, one woman from the church was keen to host a home meeting and took this piece of advice seriously. Margaret got together for moral support with a friend called Jenny. They wanted to get people in so that they had crossed the threshold before the mission week began in May, but they felt it was important to have a real reason for inviting people. So they called their event a 'Post-Christmas Blues Open House'. The two friends popped an invitation, designed by Margaret's daughter on the word processor, into their Christmas cards. Cards were handed to all fifty of their neighbours, inviting them to pop in any time between two o'clock and seven o'clock on a Saturday afternoon. Two hundred mince pies were made, nibbles and sherry purchased and then the panic set in. Despite the R.S.V.P. put on the invitation few had replied and Margaret and Jenny began to think that they would be left on their own with a mountain of mince pies. I'll let Margaret tell the story in her own words:

The day dawned, we were all ready, would anyone come? At about two fifteen the door bell rang, and from then on it was a steady stream of people popping in and out, Christians as well as non-Christians, and at some point in the afternoon all fifty people were there at one time. It was a lovely time, people found they knew each other, and those who didn't know anyone were soon engulfed in friendly chatter. I think people felt flattered to be asked. We were not on extremely friendly terms with a lot who came, just a nodding acquaintance really, so now of course we knew each other a lot better.

If evangelism is about relationships then this was profoundly evangelistic. New friendships were formed and both Margaret and Jenny were invited back into the homes of some of their neighbours. Opening our homes means opening our lives to those around us and offering to share in their joys and sorrows.

When I wrote to Margaret to ask permission to include the story, I asked if anyone had made a step forward as a result of that day. She replied, 'I don't feel anyone became involved in the mission as a direct response to the open house, but one chap who had received an invitation but couldn't come, earlier in the year lost his sister. Because we had made some sort of move in sending out the invitation, he was able to share his feelings with Jenny's husband, and did eventually make a commitment to Christ around the time of the mission.'

We need to reach out the hand of friendship and draw people into our homes and into our lives, for there Christ can be found. We need to dare to venture beyond the superficial conversations and dare to be real. Perhaps it is no accident that Margaret came from Liverpool where despite, or perhaps because of, the recession, the sense of community still runs deep. Perhaps Margaret brought with her a natural longing to build community, real community amongst her neighbours.

For evangelism to happen we need more Margarets who are

131

prepared to love their neighbours; and who realize that we must start now, and if necessary invent an excuse to get them round. We need more Caroles prepared to pray to God and ask who to invite and then be ready, no matter what the answer, to go and invite them.

BUT I DON'T KNOW ALL
THE ANSWERS

Christians strike me as being rather like greyhounds. Perhaps this analogy will be unfamiliar to the non-racegoing church member, so allow me to explain what I mean. At the start of a greyhound race, the dogs are put into the traps – a set of six narrow kennels with a door at the back, and a metal grille at the front. The dogs are shoved (sometimes reluctantly!) through the door at the back and end up peering through the metal grille which is all that prevents them making a headlong dash down the track. When the 'hare' comes past and into view the metal grille springs up and allows the greyhounds to race off and do what they are supposed to do.

When it comes to evangelism, Christians seem to be very like the greyhounds in the trap, raring to go, but with a barrier of fear preventing them getting on with the business of evangelism. If only we could remove the metal grille and get rid of some of the fear, most Christians would be unleashed for evangelistic endeavour. I say most would. I once knew a very fast and talented greyhound who possessed amazing acceleration. But after a few races she became bored and would spring out of her trap only to stop and sit down in the middle of the track, simply refusing to take part. Not every Christian is longing to get out and share their faith. Some are like that dog; though they could do it, they lack the motivation. But there are enough people in our churches who are ready and eager to do what they are called to do, if only the barrier could be raised. When teaching evangelism I frequently ask people what prevents them sharing their faith with their friends; what are the obstacles that get in the way? The answers are nearly always the same. The biggest barrier is a feeling of inadequacy; people do not feel able to argue the case for Christianity.

The biggest fear in the mind of most Christians when contemplating evangelism is of confronting an intellectual onslaught. 'I can't talk about my faith because I don't know all the answers. I need more teaching.' We are afraid that as soon as we mention our belief in Jesus Christ we will be confronted with a veritable barrage of sustained and well-thought-out arguments which we will be completely unable to answer. We shall end up a speechless little heap in the corner suffering at best a loss of face, and at worst a loss of faith.

In fact this fear is misplaced. The vast majority of people when confronted with the claims of Christianity are not argumentative – they are apathetic. In my experience 99% of the people I talk to about Christianity are either interested or apathetic. Only 1% is hostile. And with these people I quickly call it quits and walk away. Of those who are interested only a small number will be argumentative. They may come out with some of the classic objections to Christianity, but that does not necessarily mean they actually hold those views. Nor does it mean they have thought them through. John Finney's research showed that only a tiny percentage had intellectual difficulties with the Resurrection or the Virgin Birth. People had straightforward problems requiring straightforward explanations:

... there is also a widespread demand for the kind of interim apologetics which clears away the hindrances to faith for those asking simple questions at a not very profound level.[1]

You don't have to be a very clued-up Christian to outweigh the sort of opposition you are likely to come across. Most people are in the super lightweight class when it comes to thinking up good arguments against Christianity. This does not mean they don't have their reasons for disbelieving or for refusing to believe. People frequently have good reasons why they don't believe, but the reasons are usually more based on emotional arguments than on intellectual grounds: 'I don't believe because my gran died and I prayed she wouldn't.' 'I won't have anything to do with church since that vicar refused to baptize my baby.' These are the sort of objections we are likely to meet, and they will need addressing. These sorts of barriers and problems will not be brought down by intellectual argument, but by love and pastoral care. For these very real hurdles to be overcome it will require the release of emotions – anger, bitterness, hurt, fear and pain. We must wait patiently to be there to provide the opportunity for forgiveness, reconciliation and the experiencing of love. Intellectual arguments will be very secondary. And let's not forget that it is encountering Jesus that changes people. Rather than arguing them into faith, our first aim should be to challenge them to 'come and see' – to meet Jesus for themselves.

Although they will be a minority of the people we meet, there will be some who will have intellectual difficulties with Christianity and who will need good reasons given to them before they are able to believe. A large number of Christians are unable to help people who require reasons because they have a wrong understanding of what is meant by faith. It is a very common misapprehension that faith is opposed to reason.

135

People seem to think that you can't possibly give reasons for faith because faith is by definition independent of reason. Occasionally when I ask a Christian why they believe I get a reply along the lines of 'Well it's a question of faith, you have to make a leap in the dark, you've just got to believe it.' This represents a complete misunderstanding of the word 'Faith'. God does not expect us to believe in him without having a reason to do so. Faith is not a blind leap in the darkness, but a reasoned step in the light. Tragically most people define faith as meaning believing in something for which there is, and can be, no evidence. But Christian faith is not like that. Yes, God demands faith, but what He is asking for is that we put our trust in Him. He does not expect us to do that until he has shown He is trustworthy. God gives us every reason to know He is trustworthy and then says, 'Now will you trust me for the future?' Far from withholding reasons and demanding blind faith, God goes out of His way to give us cause to believe and trust Him.

Look for example at the case of 'doubting Thomas' which has so often been used to prop up this misleading definition of 'Faith'. Too often people have picked out the sentence 'Blessed are those who have not seen yet have believed'[2] while totally ignoring what actually occurs in this story. Thomas is told by the other disciples that Jesus is risen, but says that he cannot believe it without some solid evidence. Does God demand that Thomas believe just on the disciples say-so? No, Jesus comes and meets Thomas, gives him exactly what he asked for – an opportunity to check it for himself. Jesus is quite prepared to give Thomas a reason to believe.

Far from being anti-intellectual or independent of reason, the Christian faith is founded on facts. It is perfectly reasonable to be a Christian. And in his letter recorded in the

New Testament Peter reminds us that we should 'always be prepared to give an answer to everyone who asks you to give the reason for the hope that you have'.[3] As Christians we need to be ready to explain why we believe the Christian faith is true.

My first recommendation is that we prepare ourselves in advance. If you were going to court tomorrow you would obviously not just rely on the inspiration of the moment, but would prepare thoroughly. Obviously we cannot predict every eventuality but we should marshal our arguments. We need to know the reasons why we believe.

When I do seminars here at Lee Abbey I ask people to pair up and tell each other why they believe the Good News is true. When I ask people to give me their answers the vast majority of reasons that people give are subjective. They say things like 'I've had answers to prayer'; 'I felt the presence of God with me during my bereavement'; 'God has changed me and given me a feeling of peace'. These are perfectly legitimate reasons and I tell them that there is nothing wrong in giving this sort of answer, indeed it is to be recommended that we tell people first about our personal experience of God. It is this sort of warm living testimony that will excite interest in others. This sort of evidence is perfectly valid. At the heart of Christianity is a subjective experience, the meeting of a person with their maker who loves them.

But our subjective experience will need to be undergirded. Experience is a fragile thing and our spiritual experience is highly susceptible to the howling wind of doubt. Subjective experience of God will need to be supported by the reinforced steel girder of objective truth. Often our evangelism will come down to helping put up buttresses to prop up the faith born of true subjective experience.

Just as God has given us two legs to stand on and to keep us balanced, our subjective experiences need to be balanced and supported by a knowledge of the objective facts. This is important for two reasons. We need to know the objective facts which make Christianity credible, because when feelings wane and God does not seem as real, if we are relying exclusively on feelings our faith can disappear. The second reason we need the objective facts is to counteract the frequently quipped response 'Well if it works for you then it's OK, but personally I'm into . . .' We need to be able to say why Christianity is more believable than Hinduism or Buddhism. We need to be able to say why we have opted to follow the way of Christ rather than of Buddha. And the answer is given in the objective evidence provided by the Resurrection.

Buddha and Jesus both taught with clarity and beauty and both attracted followers because of this. Both claimed to be able to tell us about the meaning of life and what happened after death. Buddha said we are reincarnated, Jesus said we are resurrected. So how should we choose between them? I choose to follow Jesus for one simple reason. Jesus showed us he knew what he was talking about by dying and then coming back. Buddha did no such thing, nor do his followers claim he did. As one evangelist is fond of saying 'You come to a fork in the road. There are two men; one is dead, the other is alive. Which one do you ask to tell you the way?' Jesus is alive and can show us the way to life. Christianity is the only religion with this kind of demonstration by its founder of his credentials. Without the Resurrection, Jesus would be relegated to the second division of people who claim to have a hot line to God and claim to have understanding of the meaning of life, but whose claim is unsupported by any real evidence. The Resurrection puts Jesus and Christianity in a league of its own. The truth and credibility of Christianity hinge on the event of the Resurrection which is why you and I need to know why we believe it happened.

A man called Frank Morrison was well aware that the Christian faith rested on the Resurrection. He was not a believer and decided to write a book to disprove Christianity once and for all. He wrote his book which is called *Who Moved the Stone?*[4] The first chapter is titled 'The book that refused to be written'. In this opening chapter he describes how he examined the evidence for Christianity and found it so compelling he was converted.

We each need to take the time to look at the case for Christianity. We need to be prepared, with our reasons for believing and our faith thought out. But no matter how well you marshal your thoughts, no matter how much training in evangelism you have, you will never be able to answer all the questions and difficulties that are thrown at you. We must, in order to have intellectual credibility and integrity, be as thought-out as possible. We must do our best to answer the genuine questions and difficulties that people have. But then we must admit defeat and own up to those things we cannot explain.

I do not usually recommend that people learn Bible verses by rote. I would far rather that they quoted whole stories to make their point. But one text I do encourage people to learn by heart is . . .

I don't know but this I do know.

There is no shame in admitting when we don't know something, and we can always offer to try to find out. But we will eventually come to the limit of our understanding and we must own up to this too. When faced with something I cannot explain I copy the example of the man who had been born blind, which is told in John 9. When the Pharisees come up to

139

him following his healing by Jesus, and bombard him with questions he replies to their suggestion that Jesus is a sinner: 'Whether he is a sinner, I don't know. One thing I do know. I was blind but now I see!'[5]

I cannot explain everything, but I know why I believe. Most people who worry about knowing all the answers think that they will have to answer all of a person's difficulties before he stands any chance of becoming a believer. But the fact that they themselves are worried about not knowing all the answers proves that this is not the case. When doing seminars on evangelism I like to point out something terribly obvious but which most people miss. I ask the seminar group if they can explain how God can be three persons and yet one person at the same time. With the exception of a few smart alecs they admit defeat. I then ask them if they can answer the age-old chestnut about suffering. Again the vast majority admit to being unable to do so. I then ask them if they are Christian believers – and all say yes. I then point out to them that since they are quite capable of believing in Christianity despite not being able to understand the Trinity or solve the problem of suffering, if they can believe without having the answers to these questions, then so can other people. We do not need to solve every intellectual difficulty in order for a person to become a believer. Most of us believe despite having unresolved issues. This means that instead of trying to solve all the problems people have, we can concentrate on giving them positive reasons for believing. Just like the blind man we can say, 'I don't know. But here are the reasons I believe despite being unable to answer that'.

This idea is borne out in John Finney's research. He looked at people's intellectual problems before they came to faith and then afterwards:

It could easily be assumed that turning to God would sort out people's intellectual uncertainties for them. On the contrary the survey shows that coming to faith seemed to leave as many questions afterwards as people had before.[6]

For evangelism to be effective it does not require that we answer all the intellectual questions.

Personally I have to admit that I really struggle with the question of suffering. Oh yes I've got some intellectual arguments about free will and mankind's responsibility, and God refusing to intervene if to do so would make us robots. But though these arguments help a little bit they do not solve the problem for me. Confronted by the awesome suffering in Bosnia or Auschwitz, I find it very difficult to believe that there is a God who can answer prayers. Yet I have had answers to prayers myself. I have to admit to having reasons for doubting the existence of God, as well as reasons for believing in Him. Suffering, unanswered prayers, the rarity of the glimpses I get of Him, His obscurity, these things weigh in the balance against there being a God. When just before Christmas a couple of years ago one woman lost three children in a canal I found it almost impossible to believe that there is a God who cares. I have these doubts or difficulties and I cannot get rid of them no matter how hard I try. But the reason I am a Christian is because despite the presence of doubts, I have reasons for believing.

My faith is best described as an old-fashioned pair of scales – the sort with two pans which balance. On the one side are reasons for doubting the existence of God – at least the existence of a God who cares and who can intervene. On the other side are reasons for believing and trusting in God. I have things which sit in the negative pan of the scales and which weigh heavily against there being a God. But there are things in the positive side which outweigh them. I have had answered prayers; I have experienced the love of God and also seen it in other people some of whom have suffered greatly but none the less have maintained their faith. And the evidence for the Resurrection of Jesus sits in this side of the scales and weighs very heavily indeed.

Of all the things that I have taught in my seminars on evangelism over the past few years, it is this picture of faith as a set of scales that has had the most profound impact. More people have come up to me and commented on how helpful they find this image than have commented on the rest of my teaching put together. Why is this picture of scales describing the way we believe so liberating for our evangelism? Firstly, it means we can own up to our doubts and difficulties and share them with other people. I frequently say to people who ask me about suffering, 'I don't know and I really struggle with that problem too. It makes it hard to believe in God, but here are the reasons I am able to do so.' When I preach about the certainties of the Christian faith I see very little change in people. Whenever I am honest enough to talk about my doubts as well as my certainties then I notice people moving forward on their Christian pilgrimage.

Secondly, it means that instead of constantly trying to solve someone's difficulties we can be content to leave some of them in the set of scales against God and concentrate on outweighing them by putting other things in the plus side. We can try to give them reasons to believe despite still having their objections. Admitting that our faith is like a pair of scales can be liberating for many people who would like to believe, but who think that until their faith is 100% pure it is not adequate. All too often we act as if our faith is free of any doubts or difficulties and by doing so make it harder for people to believe. A number of people have said to me that they now feel their faith is acceptable to God despite their having some doubts.

Thirdly, the image of scales can also come to our assistance when we come to a crisis point in our faith. It can help us to assess exactly what is happening when someone's faith wobbles. For example we can lose our faith when something awful happens and as the extra weight of this tragedy falls in the negative side of the scales. To regain faith we must either remove it or outweigh it. God will help in this process, after all it is His responsibility to provide the reasons for believing. And God is quite capable of tipping the scales. I recently talked to a vicar who had taken the funeral of a teenage girl killed in a car crash. He said that for obvious reasons the faith of the family, who were on the fringes of the church, had plummeted. But then strangely their faith had deepened. Obviously the fact of the daughter's death still weighed in the negative side of the scales. But the love and awareness of God and the peace that they found actually outweighed it and their faith grew stronger.

Another way our scales can wobble and our faith be rocked is when one of the reasons for believing, one of the things that used to weigh in the plus side, is removed. Perhaps, for example, an intellectual reason that we had relied on to prop up our faith is found to be no longer credible and we have to throw it away. This frequently occurs when people go to university. Os Guinness in his book *Doubt*[7] relays the story of a young man he met whose reasons for faith were so shaky that Os Guinness suggested to him that they were unlikely to survive when subjected to the intellectual rigours of university life. Sure enough the man later wrote to him and admitted he had lost his faith. What we need to be able to do in cases such as this is help people to remove inadequate reasons for believing and replace them with good reasons. To change the analogy we have to build a reasoned faith not on shifting sand but on solid rock, so that our faith will be able to withstand any onslaught. And we need to spend time helping others to build a solid faith. To do this we must know the objective ground of the Christian faith – we need to do our homework.

The evidence is there if only Christians will bother to become familiar with it. Lord Darling, a former Lord Chief Justice, is quoted as saying:

> There exists such overwhelming evidence, positive and negative, factual and circumstantial, that no intelligent jury in the world could fail to bring in the verdict that the Resurrection story is true.[8]

Christians need to look at that evidence so they can share it with others. And Christian churches need to put on sermons and courses that sift through the facts of the Christian story.

12

MISSION POSSIBLE

The evening before writing this I drove up to Weston-super-Mare to spend a couple of hours with the team who are coming on a mission with me to a church in Torquay. Most of them are new Christians and have never been on a mission before. Understandably they were very nervous. I wanted to do everything possible to help them feel prepared and confident. We looked in some detail at the meetings we had planned to take place in people's homes, and started to discuss some of the problems and issues that people might throw at us. Far from raising their confidence the more we talked the more problems we could think of. There seemed innumerable objections people might come up with to the Christian faith and we could never cover all possibilities, or come up with enough answers. Just as I was beginning to regret the direction I had taken the vicar rescued me. 'I think we are forgetting one thing,' he said. 'We are trying to prepare ourselves and get ourselves armed to the teeth with possible arguments ready to counter all the objections that might be thrown at us. We are making it sound as if it is all up to us. Let's not forget that God is involved. His Spirit will be there communicating to them and guiding us what to say.'

I was reminded of the words Jesus said to his followers when warning them that they would be persecuted:

145

... do not worry about what to say or how to say it. At that time you will be given what to say, for it will not be you speaking, but the Spirit of your Father speaking through you.[1]

We can make the job of evangelism much too complicated. Ultimately it is not our job to convert people, that responsibility belongs to God. It is up to the Holy Spirit to do the hard work. To help people to evangelize we must lighten the load – help them to realize that it isn't all up to them, to enable them to see that the load is shared and the greatest responsibility lies with God.

In my evangelism I am not at all afraid to pass the buck. I hand over the responsibility to God. One way I do this is to get people to ask God to reveal Himself to them. A total unbeliever can pray a prayer to God asking God to show Himself, and God will honour that prayer if it is meant sincerely. I normally challenge those people who say they do not believe, but say they are interested in finding out about Christianity, to pray a prayer in hypothetical terms. I explain that without believing anything they can pray this prayer with total integrity because it includes the word 'If':

Dear God, if you are there (and I don't know that you are)
And if you care about me (and I don't know that you do)
And if you can communicate
Then please get in touch with me.
I honestly want to discover the truth.
(Based on John Stott, *Basic Christianity*)[2]

The key requirement on the part of the person praying the prayer is that last sentence. They must sincerely want to know the truth. The Bible promises that God will answer that prayer.

Without saying exactly how God is going to communicate, the Bible promises He will.

I know that this prayer works because I prayed a prayer in almost exactly those terms twelve years ago after reading the introduction to John Stott's *Basic Christianity*. At the time I prayed it I was certainly not a Christian, though I had a vague belief that there was a God out there somewhere. I had just met a Christian who made a deep impression on me, and whose faith made me start asking questions. I did not believe Christianity was true, nor did I particularly want to believe it. At least I only wanted to believe it if it was true, and I wished (as a student of psychology) to guard against any 'conversion' that was merely psychological.

I prayed that prayer at the start of the Easter Holidays 1980. Some nine weeks or so later I had moved across the divide, becoming someone who could state publicly that I believed, and was a Christian. What happened in the nine weeks to convert me? I would say nothing spectacular, no writing on the wall. Nevertheless God communicated to me in several little ways, ways that were enough to convince me, and enough to change the whole course of my life. One way was through the historical facts about Jesus. I read the rest of John Stott's book, looked for the first time at the evidence and came to the overwhelming conclusion that it was more reasonable to believe the Resurrection than to doubt it. God also communicated to me through the cartoon film of C. S. Lewis' *The Lion, the Witch and the Wardrobe*[3] which I watched at Easter and which reduced me to tears. He revealed which church it was right for me to attend through a string of 'coincidences' including a friend of a friend's car breaking down outside our house. The friend came in and invited us to come to her church. I know He honoured that prayer for me and I know He will answer it for others. Yet each time I suggest it to someone I go through a mini crisis of confidence. Will God really do anything – will He come through this time?

I have often been challenged, when recommending this approach, by people who reply, 'You say God reveals Himself – I've never seen Him. He has never communicated with me.' By way of reply I ask them to close their eyes and then to tell me either what I am wearing, or if they are not in their own home, the colour of the carpet and curtains. The vast majority of people cannot do so. When they open their eyes I point out to them that these things were before their very eyes, yet they did not see them. We are blind to so much that is around us, we just don't notice it. The same is true of God. I suggest that He has communicated to them but they have failed to see it. We need to learn to use our spiritual antennae, open our eyes to see the way God is at work. This means, of course, that one significant role we have in evangelizing people, is to help them to see what God has done and where He is currently operating in their lives. We must train their eyes to recognize the imprint of God at work, and then encourage them to co-operate with God's actions rather than fight against them.

God uses the most extraordinary ways of communicating. One of the most bizarre and powerful was to my mother. Some time after the incident of the dream (described in chapter 3 above) my mother rang me and summoned me round to her house. She lived in the beautiful rolling Sussex countryside just below the village of Hartfield in a house surrounded by fields with a river flowing along the boundary. She had a flock of fifty pedigree Suffolks, beautiful sheep with black faces. To my mother, whose children had all left home, they were like a family, she doted on them. She loved them all, but two were special. In addition to the Suffolks she had two Jacob's; a mother and her lamb. Beautiful animals with dark muddy brown coats and the characteristic shaggy wool. The pair of Jacob's were kept more like pets in the tiny field just in front of the kitchen window.

My mother told me that a dog had been worrying the sheep over the past several days, and she was particularly anxious because they were in lamb. Even if no sheep were attacked (a frightening possibility) she explained that merely being chased might lead to an abortion and lambs dying. 'Surely God cares about my sheep,' she said. 'Will you please pray that God will keep them safe?' I was only too happy to oblige, and we sat down in her little study and I prayed out loud for the safety of her sheep. I drove off home happy to have done my bit.

The next morning I got another summons, only this time my mother was in tears and sounded angry. I jumped into the car and hared round wondering what had happened. I found out as soon as I turned into her driveway. There in a wheelbarrow, upside down, legs in the air and smothered in blood, was a sheep. And not just any sheep, it was the Jacob lamb. My mother met me, her eyes still red from crying. 'Why?' she said. 'Why did God let this happen when we prayed for their protection?' I felt terrible and a failure. But then I said probably the most intelligent thing I have ever said: 'I don't know. But I believe God will tell you.' Then I jumped into my car and fled.

Two days later my mother rang again. This time her mood was all peace and calm. 'God has told me why,' she said, 'and now I'm perfectly at peace about what happened.' Once more I jumped into the car and drove round, eager to hear the end of the story. My mother explained that shortly after I had left she contacted the person whose Alsatian had been worrying the sheep. The owner denied it, so my mother called a vet and a policeman. The vet injected the dog to make it vomit, the stomach contents were examined and wool was found, proving the dog had attacked the sheep. So the dog was put down. 'You see,' my mother explained, 'you can't do anything until you can prove the dog has been troubling them. So it was worth it that one should die so that all the rest are safe.' I stared at her. This was the woman who until recently had been struggling to understand the necessity of Jesus. 'It's just like Jesus and the Cross,' I said. She looked baffled. 'Jesus was called the Lamb of God. He died so that we could be set free from the fear of death.' I showed her a passage in the letter of Peter:

> For you know that it was not with perishable things such as silver or gold that you were redeemed from the empty way of life handed down to you from your forefathers, but with the precious blood of Christ, a lamb without blemish or defect.[4]

Ever since then I have retranslated another passage in Peter's letter so it now reads:

> Be sober, be vigilant, because your enemy the devil is on the prowl like a roaring Alsatian seeking whom he may devour.[5]

I had got it right. I had promised my mother that God would tell her and He had. For my mother it had brought peace and a profound understanding of the significance of Jesus. For me it was a startling reminder that God is a God who communicates and reveals Himself to people.

In evangelism we must learn to rely on God doing the communicating, trusting that He can get through to people even if we cannot. We must lean on the doctrine of revelation which states that God wants to communicate and is quite capable of doing so. The cartoonist portrays a God who is uninvolved in His creation, sitting on a cloud passively enjoying the worship of the angels. The God of the Bible however is dynamic and active. The story of creation in Genesis, and the use of the concept of the 'Word' or 'Logos' in John's prologue to his gospel, describe a God who in His very nature is actively communicating with the world and the people He made. Paul states clearly in Romans that almost everything in the world reveals the reality of God:

> For since the creation of the world God's invisible qualities – His eternal power and divine nature – have been clearly seen, being understood from what has been made . . .[6]

God takes the initiative in making contact with us as story after story in the Bible relates: Moses was minding his own business (or more accurately his father-in-law's business) looking after sheep when God grabbed his attention.[7] There is no indication that Moses was praying or reaching out to God, or seeking Him in any way. The little boy Samuel was lying down, if not asleep, when God spoke to him. The Bible says that Samuel 'did not yet know the Lord,'[8] so it is hardly surprising that Samuel runs off thinking it is Eli who has called him. But it is not the old priest calling but God revealing Himself to the youngster. Like Samuel, God's revelation to Isaiah[9] took place in the temple, perhaps in the context of worship. Through liturgy, dreams, thunderstorms and through creation itself, God reveals Himself. In all sorts of ways, to all sorts of people God communicates. All the prophetic books contain God's message, spoken and then written down, communicating to His people. The history books in the Bible show God's actions in guiding and leading and rescuing and rebuking His people –

God revealing Himself in action as well as in word.

The story of the Old Testament is an account of God's message to us, God's word for us. It is a testimony of communication, from Heaven to Earth. The New Testament is the climax to the communication when the word becomes flesh; when God chose to communicate face to face in the person of Jesus. Knowing that His word spoken through the prophets was not sufficient to change the hearts and ways of people, God elected to adopt the most intimate form of communication possible and to come Himself. 'The word became flesh and dwelt among us'.[10] God revealed Himself in Jesus. He who was in the very core of His being God, humbled Himself and 'made Himself nothing, taking the very nature of a servant, being made in human likeness and being found in appearance as a man.'[11] It is this ultimate act of revelation, of communication that enables John to write

> 'That which was from the beginning, which we have heard, which we have seen with our eyes, which we have looked at and our hands have touched – this we proclaim concerning the Word of life.[12]

God's strategy makes sense. Suppose you had a pet tortoise (as I once did). They are quite fun little animals, but like any pet, communication is pretty limited. You can feed little bits of lettuce into their mouths and try chatting to them asking them how they are enjoying life. But there is no way you can grasp what existence is like for them. The only way you could find out, and the only way you could get through to them, would be to become a tortoise yourself. That is what God did.

If the Bible contains the story of God's communication a

couple of thousand years ago, it also contains the claim that He does the same today. God is the same yesterday, today and for ever[13] and therefore He is likely to be just as keen to communicate now as He was then. This is the practical application of the belief in the Resurrection. The Resurrection means that Jesus is still alive today. Which in turn means that we can meet Him. Pentecost and the giving of the Holy Spirit, which occurred after Jesus' body ascended into heaven, remind us of the fact that Jesus is still here and still communicating, no longer physically present but through His Spirit. We begin our eucharistic liturgy by proclaiming this glorious truth:

The Lord is here – His Spirit is with us.'

What this brief overview of the doctrine of revelation means in practical terms is that we can rely on God to do more than His share when it comes to evangelism. God wants people to get to know Him and He doesn't play hard to get. That is not to say no effort is required on our part. Jeremiah 29:12–13 should be a key text for all of us as we evangelise:

'Then you will call upon me and come and pray to me, and I will listen to you. You will seek me and find me when you seek me with all your heart. I will be found by you' declares the Lord.

This beautiful promise is restated by Jesus when teaching his disciples about prayer:

Ask and it will be given to you; seek and you will find; knock and the door will be opened to you. For everyone who asks receives; he who seeks finds; and to him who knocks, the door will be opened.[14]

What does it say we will receive? A personal revelation of God Himself. Jesus' parting shot after teaching the disciples the 'Our Father' reads:

> If you then, though you are evil, know how to give good gifts to your children, how much more will your Father in heaven give the Holy Spirit to those who ask Him![15]

It does NOT say 'how much more will your Father in heaven give good gifts' but rather 'the Holy Spirit'. The Holy Spirit is God. God will give you, in answer to your prayers, Himself. My previous boss used to sum up prayer by saying that most people's prayers could be reduced to the single sentence:

> 'Father, I have a problem – It's me!'

God's reply is always the same:

> 'My child, I have the solution – It's me.'

God comes Himself and dwells among us, ultimately within us, filling us with His Holy Spirit.

And we must lean on this fantastically wonderful truth about God's revelation when it comes to evangelism. We must remind ourselves, when talking to people about Jesus, that Jesus is there. That he has always been there working away bringing about His purposes for that person. God has, is, and will be revealing Himself to that person, and if they are open to the possibility they will come to recognize Him.

In the report *Towards the Conversion of England* the commission stated that all evangelism must be founded on a personal encounter with Jesus Christ:

> If we are to confront men and women with God, the proclamation of the Gospel must be endorsed by our own personal testimony to its converting assurance and power. Evangelists 'must be able to speak out of a genuine experience of what Jesus himself means to them . . . In the end this is the only means of an effective evangelism'.[16]

We must play our part in bringing people to that point of encounter, that meeting point with God. We must help them open themselves to the possibility of God – encourage them to seek after truth. For in seeking truth they will find Jesus who is the truth. We will need to help them not to overlook or miss the revelation of God, for in form it may be very different from what they expect. They may need our help in interpreting it and making sense of it. It is the encounter with Christ that is at the heart of evangelistic endeavour – it is its very aim.

We have made the mistake of making evangelism seem difficult. Really it comes down to something very simple: introducing people to Jesus. The passage I use more often than any other as a model for evangelism comes from John's gospel chapter 1: 35–51. Here is a classic illustration of how to evangelize naturally. Let me make several observations. Firstly, we are reminded that Christians are people who spend time with Jesus,[17] they are people who have got to know him. This is the essential qualification; for evangelism you must have a personal relationship with Jesus. Only if you do so can you possibly do what I am about to suggest.

155

Secondly, evangelism should be spontaneous, arising out of an excitement at what we have discovered;

> The first thing Andrew did was to find his brother Simon and tell him, 'we have found the Messiah'.[18]

Andrew was excited about his new discovery and naturally went straight away and told, not a stranger, but his brother. When you discover something good you naturally share it with those closest to you; your friends and family. Andrew brought his brother to Jesus and introduced them. Most of our new friends come to us by way of introduction. We take someone along to a party and introduce them to our circle of friends. I met nearly all my friends through other people. Note Andrew didn't send him off to meet Jesus, that would have been most unnatural; rather he took him, he brought him to meet Jesus. This is a vital ingredient in drawing new people into church and into relationship with Christ.

Now cynics might say that Peter was a pushover and that most people don't come along quite as easily. Which is why I like the next part of the story about Philip and Nathaniel. Nathaniel is a cynic. When Philip comes up to him and enthuses, saying that he has discovered the person they have all been waiting for [19] and it's Jesus from Nazareth – Nathaniel doesn't believe him and tries to rubbish the idea:

> 'Oh yeah, can anything good come from that dump?' (my own translation !)

Note at this point Philip doesn't rush off to his Bible and start wading through the text in order to prove his point; he doesn't get out his Ph.D. thesis showing the logical likelihood of Jesus being the expected Messiah. In fact he doesn't argue at all. He simply says, 'Come and see.'[20] An approach along the lines of 'Why don't you come and check it out for yourself before you dismiss it so quickly?' A very good challenge, which is hard for Nathaniel to refuse. If only people would adopt that as their evangelistic strategy. 'Come and see' – come and meet the living God. And before anybody snaps back and asks how can we do the same today when Jesus isn't here, let me say quickly 'But He is here'. Jesus is here by His Spirit just as He was there then physically. You can meet Him today – and our job as evangelists is to introduce people to Him. We meet Jesus today, we know the places and ways in which we encounter Him. Our job is to invite others to come and meet Him too and discover their own places where they can find Him. It is when Nathaniel meets with Jesus[21] (and not before) that he is converted – and his mind is changed. Only when he encounters Jesus can he become a follower, a disciple. We need to drop the idea that evangelism is about persuading people, arguing with them about facts, and realize that it is all about introducing them to Jesus so He can make His impression upon them.

In one sense I was a good natural evangelist at the tender age of five. It was at that age that we left our native Suffolk and moved as a family on to the Ashdown Forest in Sussex. We lived up a quiet tree-lined road called Chapel Lane, and quite naturally my mother, who had lived all her life in Suffolk, was very lonely. Being a confident five-year-old I wandered off and explored. One day soon after our arrival I rushed back into our drive, grabbed my mother by the hand and said, 'Mummy, Mummy, you've got to come with me. I want you to meet Mrs Train.' My mother was so shocked by the urgency in my voice that she obediently followed. When I got there (it was two doors up the road) Mrs Train was swinging on the children's swing, and just a little embarrassed at being caught doing so. I introduced them: 'Mrs Train, this is my mummy.' Thirty years later my mother's best friend is a woman called Diana Train. I played the part of evangelist. I had found somebody that I thought seemed really nice. Perfectly naturally, and with the lack of inhibition that characterizes five-year-olds, I went and got the person closest to me – my mummy – because I assumed that she too would want to meet this nice person. If you have met Jesus and love Him, isn't it the most natural thing in the world to go and get those you love most and take them to meet Him too?

There was no guarantee of course that my mummy and Mrs Train would get on. Nor is there any guarantee that your friends will feel the same way that you do about Jesus. But surely you cannot deny them the opportunity to find out for themselves, and the possibility of meeting their best friend. Perhaps when Jesus says we must become like little children He meant that we need to rediscover some of that lack of inhibition, so that we naturally do what is after all so positive; multiply the number of friendships that we have in the world. What more positive job could there be? Why are so many people afraid of making friends? For that is really all that we are being asked to do when asked to evangelize.

✠

POSTSCRIPT

As I come to the end of writing this book I have also come to the end of my stint as Chaplain Evangelist at Lee Abbey in Devon, and will shortly take up my next post as Rector of the small village of Dunsfold. The reaction of all my friends who are in the ministry strikes me as being indicative of how we define our role as clergy. The first question they ask is: 'How big is your new parish?' When I tell them the population of Dunsfold is approximately one thousand the response is nearly always the same. 'But what will you do?' It seems that unless there is a large number of people to baptize, marry and bury, unless there is a huge number of church groups, events and meetings to attend, ministers cannot imagine how to fill the time. Ministry has become all about doing things. I reply that I shall get to know the one thousand people who make up the community in which I shall be living. Getting to know them, love and trust them, will take time. It will certainly take time for them to get used to me and to learn to trust me.

Instead of being so busy marrying and burying people I have never met I shall spend the time getting to know the living. The fact that there are not thousands of church events every night of the week means I can join in some of the 'secular' activities and get to know those beyond the circle of regular church-goers. Instead of being rushed off my feet doing things, I shall have time for people. I am optimistic that here lies the greatest opportunity for evangelism, all the more so because the community of Dunsfold is small enough to be a real community.

What is my hope for the people of Dunsfold? My hope is the same as that of the rector of Alphington in whose church I ran my last mission as Chaplain Evangelist. The first time I met Mark Bate I asked him what he hoped might happen as a result of a Lee Abbey mission. He paused for a long while and then said: 'I would like a lot of my people to weep for love of God.' I stared at him and knew exactly what he meant. He didn't mean that he wanted some emotional hype-up. No, what he wanted was that people who came to church for love of each other, or love of the music would so encounter the love of God that they might be moved to tears in response. He hoped that the apathy that grips us all as we worship week after week would be replaced by a passionate love for Jesus Christ. That is what I hope for the people of Dunsfold and for every church with which I have had the privilege of working.

To convert people from apathy to passion will require that God sends the Holy Spirit, the Spirit of love, the Spirit of Jesus. On our part it will take the courage to allow God's Spirit to work within and amongst us, and the courage to reach out to others with love. We will need to discover the courage of people like Cathy. It is Cathy's story that gives me hope that this conversion is possible, and it is with Cathy's story that I will end this book.

Cathy was a member of the youth group that I ran in my first curacy. A quiet fifteen-year-old who took her faith seriously, and who was a regular attender of our church and of the midweek home meetings we ran for teenagers. As part of the overall evangelism of the church we encouraged the young people to bring their friends to an evening service which we had designed to be particularly accessible to newcomers. Cathy invited and brought with her a school friend, and I noticed them sitting side by side during the service. After the service I missed Cathy at the youth group, but had assumed that she had walked her friend home. It was only as I left the hall at the end of the evening that I found her crying in the lobby. 'What's the matter?' I said. It was her friend. She had sat through the whole of the service then quietly turned to Cathy and said, 'I don't think I'll ever come to church again.' Cathy had been in tears ever since. I tried to reassure her and told her she had done her bit. I reminded her that Christianity is a religion based on choice – not all choose to follow Jesus. But I went home feeling rotten and even a little angry at God for letting Cathy down. But that is not the end of the story. Three months later we had a pizza evening for the youth group, to which we had invited an evangelist to give an address. Once again we encouraged the Christian teenagers to bring their friends. Cathy with enormous guts brought another friend from school called Vicky. At the end of the evening, the speaker invited anyone who was interested to come through to an adjoining room, if they wanted to know more about Christianity. One of the people who went through was Vicky, who that night became a Christian. Cathy smiled all evening. I smile as I remember her, for there will always be hope for the conversion of this country, while there are Cathys in our midst.

NOTES

CHAPTER 1 – Mission Impossible

1 Matthew 28:19
2 John Finney, *Finding Faith Today*, Bible Society, p. vii
3 John Finney, op. cit., p. 53
4 John Finney, op. cit., p. 68
5 John 17:3
6 2 Corinthians 5:18–19
7 Ephesians 2:14–16
8 John Finney, op. cit., pp. 19–20
9 John 20:21
10 Philippians 2:5–11

CHAPTER 2 – Do you have anything to declare?

1 Thomas Aquinas, 'The Ministry and The Sacraments', p. 60 SCM, quoted in *Towards the Conversion of England*, Report of a Commission on Evangelism for the Church of England published by The Press and Publications Board of the Church Assembly, 1945
2 Matthew 28:18–19
3 Acts 1:8
4 Luke 24:47
5 Luke 24:45–9
6 Acts 1:8
7 Luke 24:49
8 John 14:26
9 John 15:26–7
10 John 16:8–10
11 John 16:13
12 Matthew 28:20

CHAPTER 3 – Honey, I shrunk the Gospel

1 The Tablet quoted in Nigel McCulloch, *A Gospel To Proclaim*, Darton, Longman & Todd, 1992, p. 81
2 Rebecca Manley Pippert, *Out of the Saltshaker*, Inter-Varsity Press, p. 78
3 *Towards the Conversion of England*, Report of a Commission on Evangelism for the Church of England, published by The Press and Publications Board of the Church Assembly, 1945, p. 36
4 *Towards the Conversion of England*, op. cit., p. 36

CHAPTER 4 – How did Jesus do it?

1 John 12:47
2 Vincent Donovan, *Christianity Rediscovered – an epistle from the Masai*, p. 61
3 Vincent Donovan, op. cit., p. 61
4 Mike Starkey, *Born To Shop*, Monarch Publications Ltd, 1989, p. 15
5 Luke 16:13
6 Alister McGrath, *Justification by Faith*, Zondervan, 1988, p. 11
7 Romans 5:8

CHAPTER 5 – His-Story, Our Story

1 Luke 1:51–5
2 Pesahim 10:4–5, cited from H. Danby, 'The Mishnah', Oxford, 1933, pp. 150 ff. Quoted in I. Howard Marshall, *Last Supper and Lord's Supper*, Paternoster Press, p. 22
3 Pesahim 10:4–5, op. cit.
4 John Finney, *Finding Faith Today*, Bible Society, p. viii
5 Matthew 7:14

CHAPTER 6 – Sharing Ourselves

1 2 Corinthians 13:5
2 1 Thessalonians 2:8
3 John 20:21
4 John 10:10
5 Ephesians 2:14–16
6 Romans 5:8
7 Margery Williams, *The Velveteen Rabbit*, Heinemann

CHAPTER 7 – Prayer

1 John Finney, *Finding Faith Today*, Bible Society, p. 35
2 O. Hallesby, *Prayer*, Inter-Varsity Press, p. 9
3 Adrian Plass, *The Sacred Diary of Adrian Plass Aged 37¼*, Marshall Pickering, 1987
4 See for example:
    The Enneagram and Prayer Barbara Metz and John Burchill, Dimension Books, New Jersey.
    Who We Are Is How We Pray – Matching Personality and Spirituality, Dr Charles Keating, Twenty-Third Publications, Connecticut
    Prayer and Temperament – Different Prayer Forms for Different Personality Types, Chester P. Michael and Marie C. Norrisey, The Open Door Inc., Virginia
5 Ruth Fowke, *Personality and Prayer*, Anvil Vol. 8, No. 3, 1991.
6 Ruth Fowke, op. cit.
7 Myers-Briggs Type Indicator
8 Ruth Fowke, op. cit.
9 Una Kroll, *The Spiritual Exercise Book*, Firethorn Press, Waterstone & Co.
10 Christopher Bryant, *Prayer and Different Types of People*, SSJE Publications, 32a Marston Street, Oxford, p. 3
11 Christopher Bryant, op. cit., p. 4
12 Christopher Bryant, op. cit., p. 5
13 Miriam Pollard, *The Laughter of God – at ease with prayer*, Dominican Publications, p. 22

CHAPTER 8 – One Step at a Time

1 *Towards The Conversion of England*, Report of a Commission on Evangelism for the Church of England, published by The Press and Publications Board of the Church Assembly, 1945, p. 36
2 John Finney, *Finding Faith Today*, Bible Society, p. 25
3 Matthew 28:19–20
4 Matthew 28:20
5 Adapted from David Watson, *I Believe in the Church*, Hodder and Stoughton, p. 47. David Watson's model was itself adapted from a model given by Prof. James Engel in *Contemporary Christian Communications*, Nelson, 1979 Nashville pp. 71–87
6 Penelope Leach, *Baby And Child*, Penguin, p. 371
7 John Finney, op. cit., p. 45
8 John Finney, op. cit., p. 44

CHAPTER 9 – Church – The Final Frontier

1 John Finney, *Finding Faith Today*, Bible Society, p. 41
2 John Finney, op. cit., p. 43
3 Theme tune to 'Neighbours', BBC1
4 Mark 12:31
5 Genesis 2. v 18.
6 Scott Peck, *The Different Drum*, Rider 1987, p. 17
7 Vincent Donovan, *Christianity Rediscovered – An epistle from the Masai*, p. 86

CHAPTER 10 – Home – The Halfway House

1 John Finney, *Finding Faith Today*, Bible Society, p. 44
2 John 17:15–18
3 Michael Wooderson, *Good News Down the Street*, Grove Books, Grove Pastoral Series No 9
   See also: Michael Wooderson, *The Church Down Our Street – A guide to everyday evangelism*, Marc, Monarch Publications

CHAPTER 11 – But I don't know all the answers

1 John Finney, *Finding Faith Today*, Bible Society, p. 63
2 John 20:29
3 1 Peter 3:15
4 Frank Morrison, *Who Moved The Stone?*, Faber 1930
5 John 9:25
6 John Finney, op. cit., p. 86
7 Os Guinness, *Doubt – Faith in Two minds*, Lion Publishing
8 Quoted in *Jesus, The Verdict* by John Young, Lion Pocketbooks

CHAPTER 12 – Mission Possible

1 Matthew 10:19–20
2 John Stott, *Basic Christianity*, Inter-Varsity Press
3 C. S. Lewis, *The Lion, The Witch and The Wardrobe*, Lions, & HarperCollins
4 1 Peter 1:18–19
5 1 Peter 5:8
6 Romans 1:20
7 Exodus 3
8 1 Samuel 3:7
9 Isaiah 6
10 John 1:14

11 Philippians 2:7–8
12 1 John 1:1–2
13 Hebrews 13:8
14 Luke 11:9–10
15 Luke 11:13
16 *Towards The Conversion of England*, Report of a Commission on Evangelism for the Church of England, published by The Press and Publications Board of the Church Assembly, 1945, p. 38, quoting William Temple
17 John 1:39
18 John 1:41
19 John 1:44 ff.
20 John 1:46
21 John 1:48–9